Telecommuting SUCCESS

A Practical Guide for Staying in the Loop While Working Away from the Office

Michael J. Dziak

With a Foreword by Gil Gordon

Park Avenue

Telecommuting Success
A Practical Guide for Staying in the Loop While Working Away from the Office

Published by Park Avenue, an imprint of JIST Publishing, Inc.
8902 Otis Avenue
Indianapolis, IN 46216-1033
Phone: 1-800-648-JIST Fax: 1-800-JIST-FAX E-Mail: editorial@jist.com

Visit our Web site at http://www.jist.com for information on JIST, free job search information and book chapters, and ordering information on our many products!

Acquisitions and Development Editor: Susan Pines
Interior Designer: Aleata Howard
Interior Layout: Carolyn J. Newland
Cover Designer: designLab
Proofreaders: David Faust, Veda Dickerson
Indexer: Sharon Hilgenberg

Printed in the United States of America
05 04 03 02 01 9 8 7 6 5 4 3 2 1

Dziak, Michael J., 1952-
Telecommuting success : a practical guide for staying in the loop while working away from the office / Michael J. Dziak ; with a foreword by Gil Gordon.
p. cm.
Includes index.
ISBN 1-57112-109-9
1. Telecommuting—United States. I. Title.

HD2336.35.U6 D95 2001
331.25—dc21 2001021255

ISBN 1-57112-109-9

You're Going to Love This Unique Book

Many books have been written about telecommuting. How is this one different?

- **Unique focus.** *Telecommuting Success* is specifically for the telecommuter employed by an organization. It discusses the issues unique to employees who work—or would like to work—away from the main office full-time, part-time, or sometimes. Other books lack this focus and try to address the self-employed, managers, entrepreneurs, and those setting up home offices. While these other readers can benefit from the information in *Telecommuting Success,* this book's distinctive focus gets telecommuting employees plugged in, productive, and promotable.
- **In-depth coverage of both tangible and intangible issues.** *Telecommuting Success* discusses in-depth all the tangible and intangible issues that concern today's telecommuter. Other books cover telecommuting technology alone or treat telecommuting as a novelty managed with basic hints. Take a look at the table of contents starting on the next page; you'll see that *Telecommuting Success* addresses all topics relevant to this increasingly popular way to work and live.
- **Self-directed and empowering.** Not only does this book explain how to become a great telecommuter, it shows you why it's important to become a "power telecommuter." This practical yet inspiring approach helps you take your telecommuting, your career, and your future into your own hands; grow in visibility and value on the job; and work with focus and balance.

The keys to *Telecommuting Success* are in your hands. Are you ready?

-EDITOR

Contents

This book is dedicated to the three loving women in my life.

Mother, Elizabeth Hamilton Dziak, my compass and my conscience.

Daughter, Jamie Catherine Dziak, my inspiration and my light.

Wife, Edna Maney Dziak, my love and my life.

Foreword

Chapter 1 of this book begins with "This Is Not Your Father's or Your Mother's Workplace," a catchy heading that introduces Michael Dziak's discussion of the diverse and sometimes convoluted changes we see in today's organizations, and the relationship between those changes and telecommuting's growth.

Ironically, as this book was going to press, General Motors announced that it plans to close its venerable Oldsmobile division in another attempt to revive GM. The media coverage about this announcement noted the most memorable recent effort to breathe new life into the Oldsmobile line—the "It's not your father's Oldsmobile" campaign of a couple of years ago. I guess that when your car brand has the word "old" as its root, you need to do something to convince today's buyers that it's not yesterday's car.

Michael Dziak's assertion that the workplace of today isn't the same as the one of our fathers' or mothers' day is much more compelling than the similar claim used by GM to disassociate from the past. In fact, Dziak has clearly made the case for telecommuting by showing not only that the workplace has changed—and will change even more dramatically—but also by proving that the question about telecommuting is not "whether" but how far and how fast it will grow.

I've known Michael Dziak since he started banging the drum for telecommuting in the Atlanta area in 1991 and have watched as his interest in telecommuting grew first to immersion and then to conviction. I can't think of anyone else who believes deep in his soul that telecommuting makes sense for employers and employees alike.

Beyond being an advocate and skilled consultant, however, Dziak has used this book as his platform to speak directly to today's telecommuter and to convey the essence of his 10 years of experience. As I went through the book, I could envision him sitting across the table from a telecommuter, imploring and guiding that person to become a "power telecommuter," as he calls it.

That's an interesting choice of words—"power telecommuter"—because it summarizes this book's purpose and value. Many books describe telecommuting, or talk about how to implement it, or otherwise very adequately cover the basics. But this book goes beyond those basics and guides you through telecommuting "graduate school"—and leaves no detail unmentioned when it comes to creating a successful telecommuting career.

This book's strength is in the countless tips, tricks, warnings, suggestions, and shortcuts that collectively mean the difference between being a telecommuter and thriving as a telecommuter. Reading this book is like walking up to the biggest, most tempting buffet table you can imagine: You see much more than you would ever think possible to consume, but you don't dare bypass anything because you know that each serving is just as good as the last.

So, sit back and settle down with this telecommuting how-to masterpiece. Michael Dziak put everything he knows about becoming a power telecommuter into it—all you need to do is read carefully, pay attention, and march full speed ahead into the new world of work we face in the twenty-first century.

GIL GORDON

Gil Gordon is founder of Gil Gordon Associates, a management consulting firm that specializes in the implementation of telecommuting and other alternative work arrangements. Gordon is an author, speaker, and noted pioneer in the telecommuting field. In 1999, he was inducted into the "Telework Hall of Fame" by the International Telework Association & Council, a nonprofit organization that promotes telework.

About This Book

Everybody knows someone who works at least occasionally from home. Telecommuting has become part of the lives of many professionals who stay highly productive without going to the office five days a week. Do you already—or would you like to—experience the freedom and rewards of working from home on a regular basis? If so, this book is for you.

This book explains how to make your telecommuting arrangements—whether formal or informal—succeed beyond your highest expectations. This book provides all you need to become what I call a "power telecommuter." It will help you learn and play by the rules of the new workplace, to use time and space to your advantage, to master the role of mobile worker, and to increase your personal and professional value as a driven knowledge worker.

Topics Covered in This Book

Telecommuters in the U.S. "have increased by an impressive 2.8 million" from the previous year, according to research findings released in October 2000 by the International Telework Association & Council (ITAC). This brings the total of telecommuters to 23.6 million nationwide.

Telecommuting is not all nirvana and fuzzy slippers. Telecommuters face challenges with time management, teamwork, and technology; with coworkers and managers; and even with family. This book shows you how to deal with those issues, plus accomplish more, communicate better, disarm skeptics, and improve your visibility, involvement, and promotability in your company—all as a telecommuter.

It is no secret that telecommuting is not at all easy. It demands a lot of work, personal savvy, and perseverance. Throughout this book, I help you understand what it takes, why telecommuters fail, and how to make sure you don't.

I discuss how telecommuters often experience incredible productivity increases, how they often do a better job and do it on time, and how, if only for brief moments, they find themselves really enjoying their work. I show you how to create a productive home environment, track your productivity, develop schedules that keep you focused, and avoid extremes of laziness and overwork.

In short, I show you how to be a power telecommuter. Now it's time for you to work away from the main office better than ever before—and this book is your roadmap.

Who Should Read This Book?

I wrote this book mainly for those 23.6 million telecommuting pioneers who work from home—sometimes without full management support. Despite the challenges, they are getting pretty good at it. Many of these telecommuters made it up as they went along and used their instincts to adapt to a remote work environment full of distractions and obstacles. These telecommuting pioneers include every remote worker—the telecommuter, the road warrior, the closet telecommuter, and even the day extender. I offer these pioneers—and all readers—a wealth of knowledge, techniques, tools, and tips on becoming a power telecommuter.

If you're currently a telecommuter: If you are already telecommuting, you can always do it better. With the knowledge and insights you gain from this book, you will. I show you how to stay connected with your customers, managers, and coworkers while you work away from the office. I guarantee at least a few "ah ha's" as I put into words what you intuitively know. The book helps you use telecommuting as a catalyst to improve your position, your skills, and your personal stock in the eyes of all who are watching.

If you wish you were telecommuting: Some sections may be overwhelming to you if you want to telecommute. But if you take baby steps and read the chapters as you need the information, this book becomes a how-to manual as you reinvent yourself as a telecommuter. At the very least, you learn critical skills that you can use right now.

If you are just entering the workforce and are interested in a telecommuting option: You are perhaps positioned better for telecommuting than any other reader. You must be patient, though. Most managers want to see unmistakable proof that you can be trusted and are capable of working without supervision. As you develop your work personality, you will find the tips on communicating with coworkers, earning superior performance reviews, career path strategies, and staying visible when you're virtual all particularly useful.

If you are a manager with telecommuters: This book offers an incredible opportunity for you to accelerate your organization's effectiveness. Even though telecommuting can be a catalyst for excellence, it will succeed only if you have effective remote work rules that are enforced equitably. This book provides you with hints on effective remote work techniques that you can use to coach employees to excellence.

If you are a manager with closet telecommuters and are concerned about telecommuting: I am pleased you are reading this. It shows you are open-minded and interested in modernizing your management skills. Looking at telecommuting from the telecommuter's perspective is one of the best ways to prepare yourself for the management of remote workers, a skill necessary in the new economy.

If you are an executive who wants an excellent telecommuting program: This book is a good start. You learn the kinds of questions you should ask about telecommuting and how telecommuting affects your employees and the organization. You learn what your telecommuters must do to be successful and the secrets of excellent remote communication. You gain the telecommuter's perspective, including the challenges they face and practical solutions to problems.

Unique Features in This Book

In addition to its helpful, detailed coverage, this book offers many unique features to help you become a power telecommuter.

Useful lists cover a wide variety of topics, including the following:

- 10 best ways to sabotage your telecommuting privilege
- Avoiding the top 10 telecommuting traps
- Mastering technology without becoming a technology geek
- Some things equipment and service vendors won't tell you
- 10 ways to prevent technology gaps and disasters
- What every home office needs—and doesn't need—for effective telecommuting
- Training yourself, your coworkers, boss, spouse, kids, pets, and neighbors
- 10 time management tips you can use today
- 10 ways to prevent stress and burnout
- Effective communication and etiquette with modern technology tools
- Developing and maintaining your telecommuting credibility
- 10 ways to stay on the corporate radar screen
- Tips from the pros on maintaining virtual relationships
- Signs that it's time to visit the main office more often
- Tips for finding a telecommuting job

Forms, worksheets, and checklists help you get organized and track your work. They include the following:

- Telecommuter attributes and accomplishments
- Mobile work task identification form
- Weekly telecommuter task and activity form
- Monthly remote work activity form

- Communication needs assessment worksheet
- Your home office checklist

Helpful sidebars discussions: These appear in shaded boxes and cover issues germane to the topic at hand.

Quotes from industry experts and relevant articles: Quotes appear throughout the book, both in the text and in highlighted boxes. They provide expert insight into key telecommuting issues.

Telecommuting resources on the Web: This special section directs you to Web sites with good information for telecommuters.

Keys terms used in this book and by telecommuters: This section allows you to look up terminology used in this book and in the telecommuting industry.

All You Need to Become a Power Telecommuter!

Once again, this book provides all you need to become a power telecommuter. It will help you learn and play by the rules of the new workplace, to use time and space to your advantage, to master the role of mobile worker, and to increase your personal and professional value as a driven knowledge worker.

Chapter 1

Working in the New Workplace

KEY CHAPTER POINTS

- This is not your father's or your mother's workplace.
- The new economy has spawned a new workplace.
- The new workplace requires a new kind of worker.
- Telecommuting is a byproduct of *and* a catalyst for the new workplace.
- Which types of employers offer telecommuting and why.
- Recognizing the primary telecommuting resistance factors.
- There has never been a better time to be a telecommuter.

This Is Not Your Father's or Your Mother's Workplace

In barely a single generation, the workplace has gone through some rather dramatic changes. Since the mid-nineties alone, we have experienced extraordinary changes in how we learn, access information, communicate, design and manufacture products, compete in business, advance in our careers, and yes, how and where we work. These changes—extremely exciting to some and most frightening to others—may feel like they have occurred in the blink of an eye.

> *"The trouble with our times is that the future is not what it used to be."*
>
> Industrial age French poet Paul Valéry

Why have these changes occurred? What impact have these shifts had on the organizations trying to remain competitive as the rules keep changing? What challenges and opportunities do these changes offer ambitious, talented professionals struggling to keep up with it all? Understanding the workplace of the past and where it is today will help you see how telecommuting fits in, why it is important to businesses and workers, and what you must do to be a successful telecommuter *and* an effective employee. This chapter addresses these and other points as it discusses working in the new workplace.

Telecommuting Is Now Part of the Business World

It wasn't all that long ago when most people had no clue what telecommuting meant. When I started in this business in 1991, it was a real ordeal to explain telecommuting. "Teleconferencing?" people would ask. Thankfully, telecommuting and teleworking have been in the press and in the workplace enough that nearly everyone now has some understanding of it.

"Workers . . . have given up on the freeway and now use the information super highway to get to work. It's called telecommuting, and it's catching on."
Tom Brokaw, *NBC Nightly News,* March 22, 1994

Here's how I explain it: Telecommuting is some combination of home-based and office-based work, facilitated by communications technology. It typically refers to an employee working at home or at another remote location away from the main office, either on a regular basis or as the situation warrants (such as when a project demands no interruptions).

"Telecommuting" Versus "Teleworking"

The term *telecommuting* was coined in 1974 by Dr. Jack Nilles, who was doing research for the University of Southern California. Telecommuting is used throughout this book for continuity, and in most cases could be replaced by *teleworking* or *telework.*

The word *telework,* also coined by Dr. Nilles, was popularized in Europe in the late eighties. Since the mid-nineties, the international telework industry has embarked on a deliberate effort to shift away from the use of telecommuting and toward the use of telework because its root implies that the primary reason for remote work is to work better and more efficiently. Telecommuting, on the other hand, emphasizes the convenience of not commuting.

When making a pitch for remote work to a skeptical manager, I recommend that you use telework. The word telework is more palatable to resistive managers because it stresses work.

Many of Today's Successful Workers Are Also Telecommuters

Throughout this book, I introduce a new term to describe the ideal twenty-first century worker. I call this person the *driven knowledge worker.* Driven knowledge workers are independent, intelligent individuals who do information-based work and are focused on success. These individuals are working at full capacity, seeing obstacles as challenges, and constantly balancing ambitious professional goals with high-priority personal and family goals. These people buy technology not as gadgets, but as tools to do what they do well even better. They are realists, recognizing the potential of today's technology to push them a little past the edge but needing regular reality checks to keep from going over that edge. These people tend to associate with those cut from the same cloth and are very interested in hearing how others deal with some of the biggest challenges they are now experiencing.

> *A knowledge worker is computer literate, has good financial aptitude, has customer care/service skills, has technical support skills, is motivated and eager to advance and learn, is drug-free and ethical, and is entrepreneurial.*
>
> Georgia Department of Industry Trade and Tourism

Because these workers use technology to the utmost, many are—to some extent—telecommuters. If you have read this far, you most likely are a telecommuter, will soon be a telecommuter, or want to be a telecommuter. This book is written to help you become even more successful at it.

You should be pleased to know that the traits of the driven knowledge worker are also those that make a telecommuter successful. That's because telecommuting takes independence, intelligence, self-motivation, and other characteristics that employers value.

Recognizing this, you can use telecommuting as a catalyst to improve your position, your skills, and your personal stock in the eyes of all who are watching. When planned, developed, and executed properly, your career and potential for growth and recognition can be enhanced if you are a good telecommuter. Why? Because, with a telecommuting mind-set, you are more efficient, you adapt better to constant change, you maximize the use of technology tools, and you can have a life outside work.

The New Economy Has Spawned a New Workplace

Technology and communications are transforming society into what is being called the *new economy,* in which the world economy, businesses, workplaces, and personal lives are morphing into something very different than we have known. "Individuals and companies worldwide are being electronically linked, a process as significant as an organism developing a nervous system," explained the editors of *Business 2.0* in the publication's premier issue. The magazine was founded in 1998 to explore the resulting revolution that is changing the rules of business. The new economy is both a catalyst for and a beneficiary of telecommuting.

This new economy is information driven. It is driven by electronically linked individuals and companies operating under new rules of time, space, efficiency, relationships, and economics. The changes from the new economy are so pervasive that they require a modernized, radical new workplace and the invention of a new employee. But what is this new economy, what is it really changing, and how is this important to telecommuters? The editors of *Business 2.0* said that the new economy has revolutionized the rules of business in the following ways:

- **Matter doesn't matter:** A company's value is found not in its tangible assets, but in intangibles: people, ideas, and the strategic aggregation of key information. This raises the value and potential of the driven knowledge worker who keeps up with technology, adapts to rapid change, and turns knowledge into profits.
- **Space is irrelevant:** Since businesses can now connect instantly with customers all over the globe, distance has vanished. This change is a primary enabler of the remote driven knowledge worker.
- **Time is collapsing:** Instant response presents incredible new business opportunities and the ability to learn from and adapt to the marketplace in real time. The reach and flexibility of the driven knowledge worker is both enhanced and expanded, for instance, by providing 24-hour support from any time zone, by being accessible at any time and from any place, and by answering e-mail correspondence after normal business hours.

- **People are the crown jewels:** Individuals who operate well under the rules of the new economy with creative, nontraditional thinking will be recognized for providing new value for their employers and be handsomely rewarded. The driven knowledge worker is in the digital driver's seat in the new economy.
- **The Internet accelerates growth:** The Internet can dramatically boost the adoption of a product or service by *viral marketing,* network-enhanced word of mouth. In the new economy, first-mover advantages are greater than ever for the organization, and the driven knowledge worker is well positioned to reap the benefits.

"In the assembly-line days, if you were slow or made a mistake, everyone knew because in that linear world, others depended on your contribution to be done correctly and promptly. Today, you could spend 30 minutes or 2 hours writing a memo, and hardly anyone would know."

Michael Dziak

- **Value rises exponentially with market share:** As more people are connected, products that help establish a platform or a standard become more pronounced. In the new economy model, some victors give away products to establish market share and then sell linked services later on. The value of the linked driven knowledge worker grows at the same time.
- **Efficiency benefits consumers:** Traditional distributors and agents (for example: brokers, wholesalers, and reservation agents) are disappearing as networked buyers begin to deal directly with sellers. In an age of information overload, a new middleman function known as an *infomediary* has emerged to provide aggregated services, intelligent customer assistance, technology-based buying aids, and community-based buying environments. Some popular infomediary services include America Online, eBay, and Priceline.com. The driven knowledge worker is well positioned to capitalize on infomediary opportunities by specializing in a field where demand for such a service is high.

- **Market models are reinvented:** Access to a network enhanced with intelligent software gives buyers dramatic new power and sellers new opportunities. New economy businesses that offer trend-setting solutions or efficiency-driven lower costs will flourish. Similarly, the connected driven knowledge worker with new economy knowledge and skills will flourish as well.
- **Transactions are enhanced by information:** The information portion of any good or service is becoming a larger part of its total value. Thus, products and services (for example: automobiles, computers, and vacations) may be customized more easily online to suit buyers' needs. Remote work transactions of the driven knowledge worker are enabled and enhanced through the same system.
- **Impulse inclinations are more easily executed:** The impulse to make a purchase, react to a crisis, or take advantage of an opportunity can be done in real time. In the online workplace, the driven knowledge worker can execute a contract, react to a complaint, or make and distribute a policy decision all at the touch of the Enter key.

Specific Changes in the New Workplace

Driven knowledge workers at all levels are the first to recognize the new economy's value and usually the first to accept the changes that come with it. And, as stated earlier, some of the biggest changes are occurring in the workplace.

Since the mid-nineties, the workplace has been going through a major transformation as a result of the new economy. This transformation involves a metamorphosis in which the traditional rules are rewritten, time and space become redefined, information and workers become mobile, and employee value is redefined.

To flourish as a driven knowledge worker in the new workplace is to know and play by its new rules, to use time and space to your advantage, to master the role of mobile worker, and to increase your personal and professional value. Take a look at some details of this new playing field:

Contrasting the Traditional and the New Workplace

The Traditional Workplace	The New Workplace Trends
Employee value is determined by tenure, years of service, and the accumulation of process, product, and industry knowledge.	Employee value is determined by contribution, talent, and fitting in, plus by the ability to find, use, and capitalize on knowledge that benefits the organization right now.
Employees are workers who report through a fixed chain of command.	Employees may also be owners and shareholders or individuals with several bosses to whom they are accountable.
A dedicated workspace is assigned to each worker, and the office's size and location delineate status in the organization.	Employees work in community or shared workspaces; some are allowed the choice of working wherever the work can be best done.
Mainframe and paper-based work information is predominantly accessible in the main office, and few work tasks are portable.	Work information is highly accessible electronically. Tasks are portable, enabling remote work activity.
Employees are specialists in their fields, independently performing their portion of the process as work flows through the organization.	Employees are specialists in their fields and involved in the entire process, contributing as a critical team member on projects typically having a defined start and finish.
Recruiting incentives include good pay, job security, and perhaps a signing bonus.	Recruiting incentives include the use of a leased automobile, stock options, highly discounted computers for personal use, telecommuting, and club memberships.
The workplace is a formal, professional place where nonwork activities and family integration are highly discouraged.	The workplace is a casual, relaxed place where work is combined with play. Some employers provide exercise rooms, on-site corporate chefs, and nature trails. Some support on-site sports competition and recreation. Employers encourage work and family balance.

The Technology Drivers

There is little doubt that we are knee-deep in the information age. Technology has given us a workplace that is very different than just a dozen years ago. We've seen the disappearance of secretaries; a dramatic increase in temporary workers, expert subcontractors, and outsourced support functions; a new car for new hires; and attention to work and family balance.

In a very short time we've added voice mail, a PC on every desk, cellular phones, high-speed digital communications, notebook computers, wireless modems, digital cameras, software on CDs, and, of course, universal e-mail and World Wide Web access from just about anywhere. By 2004, use of wireless devices, including palm devices, laptops, and Internet telephones, will increase to 29 million workers, according to a study released in June 2000 by Cahners In-Stat Group.

To make things more complicated, each organization adopts these new workplace elements as they are perceived needed, often creating a hybrid organization of old and new techniques that frequently conflict. The worker or manager who doesn't make adjustment for all these changes will be left behind. Waaaay behind.

What new workplace attributes have you noticed among the most successful companies today? Are your competitors adopting a new-workplace philosophy? How many of these changes exist in your own workplace? It's now a matter of survival. The more quickly that driven knowledge workers recognize and adopt new workplace technology and skills, the more easily they will adapt to the environment and remain competitive and successful.

The New Workplace Demands a Whole New Worker

Evidence of the workplace metamorphosis began appearing just over 20 years ago, coincident with the personal computer's introduction. Labor-intensive, paper-based workflow traditions eventually became automated, common human resource theories started becoming obsolete, and knowledge and experience once critical became useless. Through the late eighties and early nineties, hundreds of thousands of jobs were eliminated as major corporations downsized and consolidated.

The Bureau of Labor Statistics reports that in 1992 about 738,000 Americans age 55 or older were involuntarily jobless, a 51 percent rise from just five years previous. As technology advanced, many industrial-age job functions became automated, were compressed, and eliminated. Here's a sampling of job cuts that had occurred by 1993 or were announced that year:

Company	Number of Jobs Reported Eliminated
BellSouth	10,200
Delta Air Lines	3,805
IBM	60,000
Sears	50,000
Boeing	28,000

Source: Atlanta Journal-Constitution

To survive in this new workplace, the remaining workers were forced to reinvent their skill sets to match the needs of the changing organization. Survivors have had to broaden and update their knowledge base, develop a specialty skill having some value to the organization, improve analytical and computing skills, and sometimes develop a whole new work ethic. The successful new workers are among the ranks of sought-after driven knowledge workers. New workers have some advantage over their veteran counterparts since they learned many of these skills in school, yet they may lack business and workplace experience.

As discussed earlier, a driven knowledge worker is an independent, intelligent individual who is motivated to succeed. This person is working at full capacity and constantly balancing ambitious professional goals with high-priority personal and family goals. These traits relate directly to the ability to be a successful telecommuter. When such a person is telecommuting, I call this individual a *power telecommuter.*

If you have positioned yourself as a power telecommuter, congratulations! Few people fully recognize your traits, and the unenlightened wonder why you keep getting promoted over them. If you are beginning to position yourself as a power telecommuter, reading this book will put you well on your way.

What Does It Mean to Be a Power Telecommuter?

As a power telecommuter, you are not necessarily seeking power or into power trips. You are a driven knowledge worker who overcomes obstacles and achieves mastery over remote work challenges. You take the positive traits of the driven knowledge worker and improve on them through remote work.

"Power does not corrupt men," author George Bernard Shaw said. "But fools, if they get into a position of power, corrupt power." As a power telecommuter you are no fool. As a power telecommuter you

- Truly want to thrive in the new workplace and raise your proficiency level up a notch
- Get excited at the prospect of accomplishing something at the end of the day
- Look on the positive side when crises hit
- Use the remote work opportunity and technology enablers to their fullest advantage
- Recognize the times to celebrate remote work and the symptoms of its hazards
- Are clear about the type of telecommuter you are and are able to describe your telecommuting clearly in elevator conversation
- Reflect a power telecommuter persona among your friends, family, coworkers, peers, and manager

As a power telecommuter, you are more efficient, you adapt better to change, you make the most of technology tools, and you have a life outside work. Throughout the book, I discuss these abilities and how to obtain them.

Telecommuting Is a Byproduct of and Catalyst for the New Workplace

The new economy, the new workplace, and the profile of the power telecommuter are naturally suited to telecommuting. Better yet, telecommuting is naturally suited to the culture, changes, and accelerated success of organizations operating in the new economy. That's why telecommuting grew at a double-digit pace throughout most of the nineties and is becoming mainstream in the first decade of the twenty-first century.

This fit is so natural that telecommuting frequently becomes a catalyst for organizations to adopt and accelerate enculturation of the new workplace. Later on, I show you how to use telecommuting to dramatically increase your value as a quality employee in these challenging, changing times. But first, here is a brief look at telecommuting trends.

Telecommuting has passed the novelty stage. Although many employers still resist program formalization, with the rapid adoption of new workplace trends and deep proliferation of technology, telecommuting has become more mainstream in the modern workplace. James E. Challenger, president of outplacement firm Challenger, Gray & Christmas, found that 43 percent of human resource executives polled by his company said telecommuting would be the biggest workplace trend in the next decade.

The planets seem to be in alignment for telecommuting to continue its rapid growth and to become a common element of nearly every modern business in the next 20 years. The telecommuting "planets" are all in alignment:

- **Cost of technology:** High-speed, well-equipped, and complete computing systems broke the $800 barrier in 2000, and prices continue to drop. The Internet and long-distance calling are available for free, high-speed connectivity costs less than a business line, and cell phones are routinely given away—all making telecommuting affordable.
- **Economic development:** As major cities battle each other for scarce high-tech employees, the communities with telecommuting-friendly employers will attract the power telecommuters and come out ahead.
- **Management acceptance:** The number of formalized programs continues to grow at double-digit rates. Nearly all skeptical managers embrace telecommuting as a routine workplace alternative after discovering the organizational and performance benefits of a telecommuting workforce.

- **Recruiting and retention:** A shortage of quality labor and new recruits' insistence on a telecommuting option are driving more companies to allow telecommuting. And, once employers hire good people, many turn to allow telecommuting and other family-friendly options to keep them.
- **Environmental pressure:** On a smoggy day, the best way to get to work is to not get there at all. Telecommuting is the only commuter option that improves the organizational bottom line.
- **Legislation and local ordinances:** Congress and state and local governments have passed legislation that encourages or provides incentives for telecommuting.
- **Media coverage:** It seems a day doesn't go by without some mention of telecommuting in the media.

The number of American employees who telecommute from their homes to their place of business jumped to 10 percent of U.S. adults in 1999, according to research results released by the International Telework Association & Council (ITAC), a nonprofit organization that researches and promotes telecommuting. These findings imply a total of 23.6 million telecommuters nationwide. At the GartnerGroup 1999 Remote Access Conference, it was predicted that by 2003, approximately 130 million employees worldwide will be involved in telecommuting as part of their jobs.

Consider these additional telecommuting statistics:

- In the July 1999 issue of *American Demographics,* futurist author Norman Nie predicted that by 2005 at least 25 percent of the American workforce will be telecommuters or home office workers.
- A recent study cosponsored by Assurex International, a commercial insurance brokerage group, and the Educational Publishing Research Center showed that 49 percent of surveyed employers offer a compressed or alternative workweek, 32 percent allow telecommuting, and 23 percent offer a job-sharing option.
- According to International Data Corporation, in 1999 there were 37.3 million home office households in the U.S., of which 7.8 million had more than two PCs.

- By 2002, the number of home office households with local networks is expected to skyrocket to more than 8 million, according to International Data Corporation.

Which Types of Employers Offer Telecommuting and Why?

Although organizations with telecommuters share some common traits, it is nearly impossible to comfortably pigeonhole them in any major way. They are very large to very small. They are public sector and private sector. They are privately owned and publicly traded. They are high-tech information intensive and low-tech manufacturing. They are constantly boasting about their telecommuting success to get good press, or they refuse to talk about it for competitive reasons. What they do have in common is a recognition that telecommuting can be highly beneficial to employers and employees alike.

Telecommuting Benefits and Proven Results

Telecommuting Benefits	Proven Telecommuting Results
Reduces employee absenteeism and turnover	Employees who telecommute can annually save their employers $10,006 each in reduced absenteeism and job-retention costs, according to research announced in October 2000 by ITAC.
Improves employee performance	Employee performance increases due to working during peak periods, uninterrupted work time, and other factors. The Colorado Telework Coalition says American Express telecommuters produced 43 percent more business than office workers; Compaq productivity increases ranged from 15 to 45 percent.
Provides operations contingency options	Telecommuters can remain productive during inclement weather, unexpected traffic congestion, utility failure at headquarters, or by being available to meet unexpected call center demand.

Telecommuting Benefits	Proven Telecommuting Results
Meets federal requirements	A telecommuting organization can more easily comply with requirements of the Americans with Disabilities Act, the Clean Air Act Amendments, and the Family & Medical Leave Act.
Increases profits and improves competitiveness	Telecommuting can act as a catalyst for improving operating efficiencies, internal communication, management skills, overall competitiveness, and the use of existing and emerging technology tools.
Improves employee quality of work/life	Telecommuters experience reduced stress by having more quality time with family and by eliminating their commute on telecommuting days.
Enhances the benefit of strategic initiatives	Telecommuting is highly complementary to operations improvement initiatives, such as quality management, reengineering, teamwork, and the paperless office.
Reduces real estate costs	Real estate costs may be reduced where office sharing and full-time telecommuters exist. According to telecommuting author and consultant Gil Gordon in his newsletter, *Telecommuting Review,* IBM US reduced real estate costs by 40 to 60 percent. The Institute for the Study of Distributed Work says $8,000 per worker can be saved yearly in office space expenditures.
Improves employee computer literacy	Telecommuting forces employees to become more proficient at the use of telecomputing equipment, increasing an individual's value as an employee.
Expands quality employee recruiting	By offering a telecommuting option, organizations can attract high-quality or specialist employees interested in a remote option or who reside outside the normal commuting

(continues)

(continued)

Telecommuting Benefits and Proven Results

Telecommuting Benefits	Proven Telecommuting Results
	distance. Fifty-three percent of telecommuters say the ability to work at home is important to their employment choice, according to ITAC.

"Many analysts predict that in the not-so-distant future, most white-collar workers will be entirely mobile. Instead of spending time in a corporate office, they will work alongside employees from other companies in telecenters that are equipped with faxes, copiers, computers, and administrative help."

Daintry Duffy, "Cube Stakes," *CIO Enterprise*, April 15, 1999

Telecommuting has reached a critical mass among employers. As noted earlier, 32 percent of the human resource professionals responding to a survey cosponsored by Assurex International and the Educational Publishing Research Center say they allow telecommuting. The latest statistics available show that in 1997, up to 25,000 federal workers—which is about 1.5 percent of the federal workforce—were telecommuting nationwide, and the government is aiming to have 15 percent working from home by 2002. Many state and local governments have adopted a telecommuting program. For a good list of some employers with telecommuting programs, see telecommuting author and self-proclaimed "televangelist" June Langhoff's Web site at www.langhoff.com/companies.html.

As long as the economy remains strong, organizations will be adopting telecommuting for three primary reasons:

1. To recruit and retain quality employees
2. To solve a specific problem that threatens the organization's success (office space at capacity; low employee morale; lagging employee productivity; absenteeism in core departments; no more parking spaces; to enhance other strategic initiatives; poor customer service; and so on)
3. To reduce costs and improve operating efficiency in a major way

The bottom line is that organizations invest in telecommuting for its profound effect on, well, the bottom line. As a power telecommuter you can be no better positioned than working for an organization that is serious about telecommuting.

Recognizing the Primary Telecommuting Resistance Factors

Not all organizations embrace telecommuting. It's a well-documented fact that most obstacles to successful telecommuting are more psychological than technological. Likewise, telecommuting programs are far more prone to failure for management reasons than for technology reasons. In an organizational culture entrenched deep in industrial-age tradition, formalized telecommuting can appear to some as radical as flying cars.

The authors of an interesting study released in 1998 by the GartnerGroup predicted that "Half of the first-time remote-access pilot programs will fail," citing a variety of nontechnical reasons. So far, the telecommuting industry has not confirmed that this has occurred. But it does confirm that the potential of a telecommuting investment depends greatly on executive commitment, proper program development, and effective measurement of program results.

> *"Alternative office designs fail for the fundamental reason that companies are making an investment in the facilities planning and the IT infrastructure to support a new strategy—but not in the employees who will be most affected by it."*
>
> Daintry Duffy, "Cube Stakes," *CIO Enterprise*, April 15, 1999

For your employer to run a successful telecommuting program, management must do two things:

- Invest in processes, facilities, tools, infrastructure, and quality employees.

- Fully prepare employees for these changes by providing continuous education.

As with any major change, there will always be those who resist this new workplace culture. If your organization is resistive, successful telecommuting will take a lot more work on your part (which I cover in Chapter 5). If you are faced with this obstacle, it may help to understand the core of this resistance.

Executives resist telecommuting when they imagine empty offices and the high cost of duplicating electronics. Managers resist telecommuting when they imagine not being able to see their workers busy at their desks. Although these and other misconceptions can be overcome with the proper development and implementation of a telecommuting program, they still constitute a genuine roadblock to telecommuting. Here are the primary reasons that telecommuting is resisted by management and what you can do about them:

- **I can't tell if you're working if I can't see you:** Before computers, a manager could take a quick glance at a worker's desk and tell if at least some work was being done. Nonwork activities were pretty obvious and hard to hide. Many desk jobs became the paper extension of a countable-task factory environment (processing claims and sales orders, for example, where output could be quantified). The prevailing philosophy was (and unfortunately still is in many cases) that if you were at your desk or at a meeting under the observation of others, you must be working. If you weren't around, you must be goofing off. Today, it's difficult to distinguish work from leisure just by looking. If managers have not updated their skills, then telecommuting is perceived as a threat to their ability to manage. **Antidote:** Keep good records of your telecommuting days, time, and work activity. Go out of your way to tell your manager exactly what you accomplish during each telecommuting event. See Chapters 2 and 6 for more on this.

"The office is designed for 'work,' not productivity. Work can be defined as 'anything you'd rather not be doing.' Productivity is a different matter. Telecommuting substitutes 2 hours of productivity for 10 hours of work."
Scott Adams, *The Dilbert Principle*, HarperBusiness, 1997

- **I won't be able to call a meeting:** In my company's client survey work, this response is consistently among the top three management concerns. Uninitiated managers imagine that telecommuting will empty their workgroup, leaving them with no one to call to a meeting. **Antidote:** Short of simply reducing the number of meetings, your options are limited. If impromptu meetings are important to your manager, you will need to remain reachable and sometimes even have to drive to the office to attend them. Except under extreme circumstances, meetings can be effectively attended by speakerphone or teleconference. It will be up to you to make the technical arrangements and establish a comfort zone to assure this method works. If workgroup representation at meetings remains an issue, you may have to coordinate with your coworkers to limit the number of telecommuters who are out at any given time.
- **There's no budget for equipment and services:** This is a common concern of skeptical managers looking for a reason to avoid telecommuting employees. Although proper telecommuting requires connectivity, it can be done on a low budget. **Antidote:** Individuals interested in (and qualified for) telecommuting should be prepared to make a personal investment in proper equipment and services to get the job done. A solid business case, however, can be made for a substantial corporate telecommuting investment as long as management can quantify the return on investment.
- **Workers who shouldn't be allowed to telecommute will want to:** This excuse is possible evidence of weak management skills. There is little doubt that some employees will look at telecommuting as an opportunity to work less and get away with it. **Antidote:** One of the first things you should know about telecommuting is that it is not for everyone. Only those who meet strict job, tenure, and performance criteria should be allowed the privilege. If your manager remains nervous about your telecommuting, find out why and do your best to overcome it. Some ideas are offered in Chapter 2.

When a telecommuting program fails, it is not likely caused by telecommuting itself. The truth is, telecommuting fails among larger employers when it amplifies preexisting organizational problems such as poor internal communication, low morale, unhealthy competition among departments, weak performance measuring techniques, mistrust of management, and poor leadership and management skills.

If you work for a smaller organization, are trusted to do your work, and communicate fairly well with your manager, these weaknesses will have less effect. The larger the organization, the more important it is to have formalized rules, well-trained participants, and telecommuter accountability.

The good news is that telecommuting can actually help solve organizational weaknesses, only if management admits to the problems and is willing to invest in the solutions. I talk more about how to make your manager less nervous about your telecommuting in Chapters 2 and 6. If telecommuting is resisted due to preexisting problems, don't give up hope. Telecommuting might just become the catalyst for overcoming them.

People Have Been Working from Home for Thousands of Years

Working *away* from home is a relatively new and novel thing. Did you know that the traditional workday and separation of work and home have been around for a fraction of the time humans have been on Earth?

- In primitive times, hunters and gatherers primarily depended on wild food for sustenance, migrating with the seasons, but working at or near home for thousands of years.
- In the agrarian age, which began more than 400 years ago, farming settlers primarily depended on agriculture and domesticating animals for sustenance, living and working primarily at home.
- It was during the industrial age, which began just over 100 years ago, that for the first time large numbers of people began living *away* from work. Workers were paid for laboring in factories and offices, and they lived in urban and suburban areas near or easily accessible to work by transit or car.

Only in the last 10 years have huge numbers of workers transitioned back to the home for work. For reasons explained earlier in this chapter, there's been a surge in part-time and full-time telecommuters, mobile workers called *road warriors,* and home-based businesses.

There Has Never Been a Better Time to Be a Telecommuter

With new technology, the new workplace, and new information-age opportunities brought on by the new economy, the demand for power telecommuters will continue. In summary, here's why there has never been a better time to be a telecommuter:

- The traits of the sought-after new employee and the successful telecommuter are virtually the same.
- Telecommuting is a byproduct *and* a catalyst of the new workplace.
- Readily available technology tools are safely and economically extending the workplace more than ever before.
- The planets are in alignment for rapid growth and popularization of telecommuting.
- Telecommuting has transitioned from an interesting novelty to a proven business tool for improving the organization.

The stage is set. Being a power telecommuter dramatically increases your value as a quality employee in these challenging, changing times.

The rest of this book steps you through the process of becoming a power telecommuter. Much of what you read you probably know intuitively. You probably already do some of it. Most of it can be put into action right away.

Much like a professional musician in an orchestra, as a power telecommuter you must become highly practiced and professional, have a unique style of working, have a personal definition of job satisfaction, and yet blend well with the rest of the group.

"Organizations are becoming contingents of independent agents, forming self-managing teams," according to Duncan Sutherland, chief technology officer of the Washington, D.C.–based law firm Wilmer, Cutler & Pickering. "Individuals are empowered with knowledge of the mission, cognizance of their role and responsibilities, and all following the same sheet music, much like an orchestra."

Being a power telecommuter means you will play a key role in the orchestra, but you'll always be reading from sheet music that's a little bit more complicated than the others. It's time to begin the journey by learning how you can best establish, position, and solidify your telecommuting integrity.

CHAPTER 2

Positioning Yourself As a Power Telecommuter

KEY CHAPTER POINTS

- Learning the keys to telecommuting success.
- If you are not allowed to telecommute now, here is guidance on making your case.
- Why you should consider elevating your persona to power telecommuter.
- Tracking, measuring, and reporting your work.
- 10 ways to sabotage your telecommuting privilege.
- Avoiding the top 10 telecommuting traps.
- Making your "telecommuter pledge."

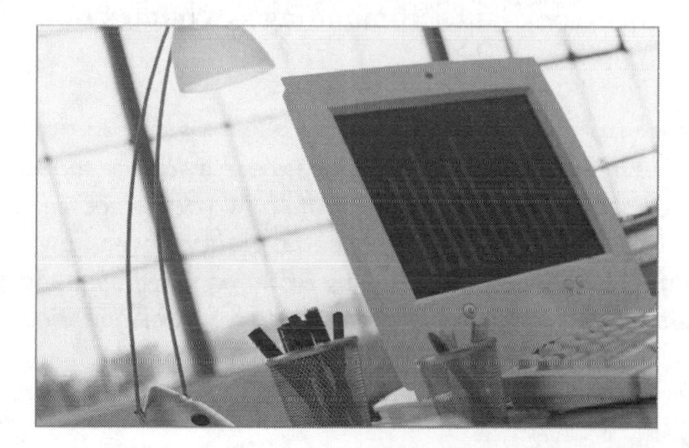

Learning the Tangibles and Intangibles of Telecommuting Success

Successful telecommuting takes a lot of work. In this chapter, I show you the reasons for and steps to establishing yourself as a power telecommuter, the bedrock position for everything you do in this role. After explaining the upside and downside of telecommuting, I help you develop a work mode that meets your manager's approval, clearly identify your telecommuter type and profile, create obvious value in your work output, shun self-destructive behavior, hurdle obstacles with finesse, avoid common traps, and keep remote work in perspective. By the end of this chapter, you will be prepared to commit to telecommuting success by making the "telecommuter pledge."

If You Are Not Allowed to Telecommute, Here's the Guidance You Need to Make It Happen

While many people picked up this book to become more successful as telecommuters, I realize that other readers, for one reason or another, are not formally allowed to telecommute. If you are not telecommuting but would like to, the first section of this chapter is for you. Current telecommuters may wish to skip to the section titled "If You Are Already Telecommuting."

As I point out in Chapter 1, telecommuting is byproduct of and a catalyst for the new workplace. But what do you do if your workplace isn't "new" at all? What if management looks at telecommuting as a burden or thinks it is a way for people to do less work?

"Present your manager with solid business-case evidence supporting your telework arrangement. Clearly demonstrate how your telecommuting activity will satisfy organizational and work needs, perhaps even how it will solve nagging organizational problems. In my experience, when managers finally recognize there is something in telecommuting for them, lingering doubts are replaced with the bliss of enlightenment."

David Fleming, founder and president of Fleming LTD, a telework consulting firm

If telecommuting is not formalized in your organization with policies, procedures, and training, you will have to find a way to show your manager that telecommuting will not only improve your performance but will make the manager look better. You may even have to instigate a formal program. While this seems like a monumental task, I have seen some large organizations establish a companywide formal telecommuting program as a result of one individual's persistence.

Although I don't expect every reader to have these kinds of ambitions, it is important to understand that under some circumstances, if you want to telecommute, you may have your work cut out for you.

Take a Walk in Your Boss's Virtual Shoes

With a little information and a lot of patience, you can persuade even the most skeptical managers to support telecommuting. One of my first clients had an army of skeptical managers. In operation for nearly 100 years, this major corporation had many veteran managers who believed "All our employees need to be at their desks to do their work" and "Remote work is not something we can do here." Sound familiar?

Once I identified and neutralized the skeptical managers' basic fears and created an environment in which these managers believed they could maintain control over telecommuters, most of these skeptics became the company's biggest telecommuting supporters.

If you report to a skeptical manager and you want to telecommute, you need to take a walk in this person's virtual shoes. What are the real reasons your manager is against telecommuting? What are the actual concerns and obstacles? If you place yourself in your boss's position and construct the concerns he or she may have, it will become obvious that most are based on "false evidence appearing real" or "FEAR," a concept used by David Fleming of Fleming LTD in his telework training.

Here are questions a skeptical manager may ask and some ways to eliminate the "false evidence":

- **Why do you really want to telecommute?** Even if your personal motivation is to spend more time with your family or reduce commuting time, your answer should focus on the benefits to your work performance, your manager, and to the organization. It is critically important at this stage to be prepared to explain how telecommuting will allow you to achieve certain work tasks or complete specific projects more quickly and more efficiently, to save money, to improve customer service, or to offer some other benefit to the organization.
- **How often will you telecommute?** Assure the boss that you are not going to disappear. The average telecommuter works from home once or twice a week. If time away from the main office is a real concern, you might begin telecommuting half days, working on a task at home in the morning and coming into the office after lunch.
- **Why should you be allowed to telecommute?** Develop a list of ways your work output will improve through telecommuting. Scan the Web for common telecommuting benefits, statistics, and trends that are pertinent to your situation. You could also identify a few employers in your industry or community that offer telecommuting and show how the organizations benefit.

"Making a business case for the option to telecommute will only merit consideration if the argument does not appear to be self-serving. The organization has to benefit, or the effort is wasted."

Eddie Caine, professional services manager for TManage, which designs, develops, and manages large-scale employee telework programs

---

- **What kind of work will you be doing at home?** Explain that you will be working on hot projects and priority activities that require quiet concentration. At least in the beginning, plan on working at home only when you have a specific reason (to finish a project, complete a report, contact customers in a different time zone, and so on).
- **What will you do if you run out of work at home?** Assure the boss that you will carry tasks that can be accomplished wherever you are. Describe how you will keep a satchel with remote work projects that

you can focus on when you have to telecommute unexpectedly, such as when there's a bad traffic accident in the morning, an ice storm, or a smog alert day.

- **What if everyone else in the office wants to work at home?** This is one of the most potent obstacles to telecommuting. Without telecommuter selection criteria and remote work guidelines, it will be difficult for managers to decide who should and shouldn't telecommute without stirring up controversy. Make the suggestion that only individuals with portable work tasks, a minimum of six months in their positions, acceptable home conditions, and excellent or superior performance ratings be allowed to telecommute.
- **How will I know you have actually been working?** This is where you put your excellent communication skills to work! Explain that before you bring work home, you will sit down with the boss and review exactly what you will accomplish. You will do the work at home and, when you return, you'll show what you did. Later in this chapter I show you some ways to keep your manager well informed on your remote work activities. You may want to regularly accomplish more than agreed as insurance to allow continued telecommuting.
- **How will I reach you when you're at home?** You must remain reachable, otherwise any trust you build can be destroyed after just one "I couldn't reach you at home" incident. Be sure that the boss has your home number and the numbers for other ways of reaching you, such as by a second line, a mobile phone, or a pager. Explain that you occasionally take breaks away from the phone, but you'll call back within an hour. When you need uninterrupted time, record a voice mail that will set expectations for returned calls.
- **Who will be taking care of the kids?** Assure your boss that your child-care situation will remain the same and that you will not be caring for children or dependent adults during working hours. Family responsibilities and work responsibilities generally do not mix, so make accommodations accordingly. In some instances, however—such as where work output can be clearly measured—a telecommuter can work while a child is sleeping or when the other parent comes home.

- **What if I need you here in the office?** If a crisis or unexpected meeting requires your presence, the boss should know that you are willing to drop what you are doing and be there. Ideally this won't happen very often. To reduce such possibilities, you may want to make arrangements to have speakerphones installed in conference rooms so that you can virtually attend important meetings.
- **Is your home a good environment for work?** It is important for the boss to visualize your home office as a professional environment. Provide your manager with a detailed description of the room or area, supported with a drawing or photo, to create the appropriate mental picture. You could also list the major technology tools you will be using and how you intend to safely move work back and forth.
- **Who's going to pay for all this?** Don't expect your employer to pay for your entire home office. If you are serious about telecommuting, you may need to make a personal investment. Eventually, as the telecommuting program is formalized, the organization may offer surplus equipment or furniture and reimburse you for an extra telephone line and other business expenses.

This is a sampling of the questions that your manager may ask. Since you know your situation better than anyone, put yourself in your manager's shoes, anticipate as many questions as you can, and be prepared to answer them.

"If your organization isn't well along the way in learning how to accept and use flexible work arrangements and in giving managers skills at leading rather than bossing, you're going to have difficulty attracting and motivating this generation."

Gil Gordon, Gil Gordon Associates, *Telecommuting Review,* February 1998

If You Are Already Telecommuting

Telecommuting or not, you owe your manager certain information about your work output, how you spend your day, and work tasks you have accomplished. If you already telecommute occasionally and don't regularly present work you're doing at home, or if there is no set pattern on how you keep in touch with the office, you need to start right now. With this simple communication, even the most skeptical manager on the planet can become more open-minded about remote work.

Setting Up a Program

So now that you've educated the boss and reduced the "FEAR" factor, it's time to set up a company program, right? If you are ready to take it on, go for it! This is often one of those cases in which the impossible just takes a little longer. The following sidebar provides an overview of what it will take. You will need management's help throughout the process. If developing a company telecommuting program is something you cannot do for whatever reason, the following information should still be useful to you and your manager.

The Steps to Telecommuting Program Development

Over the past 20 years or so, a standard practice has emerged for effective telecommuting program implementation. Although it might at this point be tempting to take shortcuts, telecommuting history is littered with failed programs because of such shortcuts.

Borrowing concepts from the Metro Atlanta Telecommuting Advisory Council (MATAC), I list the eight steps to developing a telecommuting program in your organization. Details of this step-by-step guide can be found at the MATAC home page, www.matac.org, by clicking on "How To" and then "Set Up Program." Note that for smaller organizations, the amount of formality you need is commensurate with the trust level between employees and managers. The more trust, the fewer rules.

1. **Purpose:** Establishing a clear purpose is often the first challenge in developing a successful telecommuting program. The purpose of the program, which must serve a business need (such as improved recruiting and retention, reduced overhead costs, improved customer service, or meeting federal requirements), will drive the program personality, budget, focus, organizational penetration, and success.

(continues)

(continued)

2. **Preparation:** The next step is to design a solid foundation on which to build the program. In the preparation phase, the personality and success factors of a program are formed and implemented. Volunteer to lead a task force to explore telecommuting, obtain baseline information about the employees, and prepare a pilot program plan.
3. **Plan:** Once the program goals are finalized and approved, the planning process begins. The plan will be the roadmap that governs implementation, participation, and rules of engagement. It should provide checks and balances and tools for measuring progress and increase the potential for long-term success.
4. **Participants:** Proper selection and training of telecommuting participants are critical. After being selected using participant criteria, telecommuters–along with their managers and even their coworkers–should be oriented through training and provided with the purpose, policy, and procedures to successfully participate in the program.
5. **Perception:** Many obstacles to remote work programs involve not the technology but the psychology of telecommuting. For an organization to successfully adopt a program, it is critical that executives, management, employees, customers, and sometimes the public have a clear understanding of its nature and purpose. Creating an accurate perception of telecommuting purpose, benefits, and results will assure support and acceptance.
6. **Pilot:** Experience shows that organizations embarking on a telecommuting program should start with a small, representative sample of telecommuters to test the policy, procedures, and systems, and to determine if the goals set by the task force are achievable. Pilot programs can last from two to six months and should be fully documented and closely managed.
7. **Performance:** Successful telecommuting programs start with measurable goals and objectives. How will you know if the program is successful? It is critical that the organization develop metrics for measuring program costs, employee attitudes, performance changes, travel time and miles saved, training effectiveness, customer perceptions, and other elements to measure success.

8. **Permanence:** A telecommuting program, if planned, designed, and implemented properly, will become a permanent, beneficial element of the organization. Ultimately, the goal should be for telecommuting to become as common and accepted as any other organizational policy or program.

Why You Should Consider Elevating Your Persona to Power Telecommuter

By the time you finish this book, I would like you to have positioned yourself as a power telecommuter among your friends, family, coworkers, peers, manager, and organization. A power telecommuter is a self-disciplined mobile worker who requires minimal supervision, is a skilled communicator, balances work and personal life, is an independent team player, manages time well, and stays in the loop while working away from the office.

As a continuation of the "new worker" discussion in Chapter 1, I want to highlight what it takes to thrive in today's workplace. After that, as a reality check, I discuss the benefits and pitfalls of telecommuting. Then I help you clearly define the kind of telecommuter you are or want to be so that your personal telecommuting "persona" is clear. Finally, I show you some steps to making, posturing, and solidifying your telecommuter pledge.

What It Takes to Thrive in the New Workplace

You may notice that many of your peers are satisfied with just surviving or merely existing in the work environment. Some put in a full day and complain about conditions and problems, but they don't seem willing to invest the energy to get ahead. You often see people doing more "existing" as they get closer to retirement.

Others look at their job as just a job—a begrudgingly boring way to do the minimum to keep the paycheck coming in. These people hate the thought of going to work, complain about anything that doesn't go their way, can't wait for Fridays, and sing extra loud when the song "Take This Job and Shove It" comes on the radio.

However, driven knowledge workers like you put in a little extra toward each task and take pride in doing what you do well. You don't necessarily love to go to work but get excited at the prospect of accomplishing something by the day's end. You look for the positive side when crises hit and do the best work you can with the tools you have.

Someone once told me that it takes just as much energy to have a bad life as it does to have a good one, so why not put positive energy into everything you do? That's the kind of attitude people like you have, the "half full" kind of people, the ones who want to thrive and not just survive in the new workplace.

But it takes work. If you really want to thrive in the new workplace and raise your level up a notch, you must be

- **Adaptive and willing to change:** One thing you can be assured of in the new workplace is change. To thrive, you must anticipate change and take advantage of anything new to gain a competitive edge.
- **An excellent manager of information:** Twenty years ago, futurists were promising the elimination of paper in the office. As you know, the opposite has happened: We generally have more information and paper than we know what to do with. As information access continues to grow exponentially, you must select and use resources and media that complement your mission and maximize your efficiency.
- **The ultimate entrepreneur:** Whether you are employed by a multinational company or work as an independent contractor, the new workplace enables the individual to do the work of many. As the ultimate entrepreneur, described in *Fortune* magazine as early as 1994, "you deliver skilled services with far less overhead than bigger providers." As a result of technology, the ultimate entrepreneur becomes a highly skilled network security consultant, a successful Web page designer, an industry magazine or corporate newsletter publisher, and a specialty product designer or a building architect, exploiting opportunity and always positioning for more.
- **Empowered as a team player:** A paradox in the new workplace is operating as the ultimate entrepreneur yet remaining a team player.

As organizations become more project-oriented, it is even more important that you simultaneously contribute as an individual and complement the team.

- **A specialist critical to the organization:** Your worth is increasingly measured by your ability to provide value as a self-directed team member capable of carrying out specific functions better than anyone else.
- **An excellent communicator:** None of the above qualities has any real value without the ability to communicate well, both socially and electronically. To thrive in the information age, you must become a master of the written and spoken word and a master user of the technology that carries it.

These challenges stand before anyone who wishes to thrive and not merely survive in the information age. These thriving traits are also key traits of the power telecommuter.

Some Telecommuter Realities: Common Benefits and Pitfalls

From the outside looking in, telecommuting may seem like the perfect work arrangement. It offers you freedom, independence, flexibility, and plenty of upside benefits. However, telecommuting has its share of downside pitfalls. By knowing and avoiding the common telecommuting pitfalls, obstacles, and temptations, you have a much better chance of becoming and remaining successful. As you develop your telecommuting persona, make sure you give strong consideration to both sides of the equation.

The Benefits and Pitfalls of Telecommuting

Telecommuting Benefits	Telecommuting Pitfalls
The quiet environment allows full concentration.	Isolation from coworkers can change your relationships.
You can often set your hours and work during your peak performance time.	It's easy to be lazy and become distracted from your work.

(continues)

(continued)

The Benefits and Pitfalls of Telecommuting

Telecommuting Benefits	Telecommuting Pitfalls
You may be recognized for improved quantity and quality of your work output.	You could be passed by for a promotion because of your low main-office profile.
The monetary and mental costs of commuting can be significantly reduced.	You should expect to bear the cost of some equipment and services.
There are fewer interruptions by coworkers.	You can find yourself out of the workplace loop.
It is possible to work while recovering from an illness or injury.	Going back to work too soon could prolong recovery from an illness or injury.
Commuting time is eliminated.	You tend to work during the time you'd be commuting.
You spend more time with family because you are home.	You spend more time with work because work is at home.
Manager trust can improve significantly with good communication.	Trust can be lost with one incident.
Others admire the telecommuting privilege.	Others envy the telecommuting privilege.
You can eat meals whenever you want.	You can eat meals whenever you want.

A power telecommuter uses remote work benefits to full advantage and is constantly avoiding the pitfalls. As a power telecommuter, you learn to recognize the times to celebrate remote work benefits and recognize symptoms of its hazards. The best way to do this is to invent a personal telecommuting profile and project it into everything you do.

Inventing and Projecting Your Telecommuter Persona

Telecommuting has reached such a critical mass in the United States that nearly everyone knows someone who is doing it. But, as you probably know, there are different types of telecommuting and varying degrees of telecommuting proficiency.

As a power telecommuter, you must not only be clear about the type of telecommuter you are, but you must be able to describe it clearly in elevator conversation. This requires that you establish your telecommuting persona and craft a quick description that you can repeat consistently. An example of such a description would be "Yes, I'm a telecommuter. I work at home two or three times a week to work on projects requiring full concentration."

> *"Make believe you're crafting a business plan for doing your job and achieving specific performance objectives as effectively and efficiently as possible."*
>
> Warren Master, director of public management consulting at the accounting firm Clifton Gunderson

Using the following table as a guide, take a moment to determine the type of telecommuter you are or would like to be and then key in your profile on a blank page. Read it out loud a few times, change it, and make it perfect. This way you will clearly know your telecommuting persona.

Once you have described your telecommuting type, take a moment to affirm the personal and positional traits that make you eligible for the privilege of telecommuting, and then list the actions you have already taken to assure your telecommuting success. Finally, at the end of this chapter, make your telecommuting pledge to finalize your commitment as a power telecommuter.

Telecommuter Type

As a power telecommuter, I

- __ Work from home part-time
- __ Work from home occasionally

  Frequency:
  - __ less than six times a month as needed
  - __ two to three times a week as needed
  - __ to __ times each week on specific days of the week
  - __ Other ______________________________

or

- __ Telecommute full-time under the following conditions:
  - __ As a road warrior from a virtual office
  - __ With my home office as my primary workplace, working in the main office as needed
  - __ With my home office as my primary workplace, working in the main office on rare occasions

and

  - __ I share workspace with others when I work in the main office
  - __ Other ______________________________

Telecommuter Attributes and Accomplishments (check the ones that apply to you)

The traits I have that are desirable for telecommuting include

- __ A position with portable work tasks that can be accomplished remotely
- __ Being a self-starter with an excellent or superior performance history
- __ Knowing my organization's mission and vision and how I fit into it
- __ Possessing enough experience on the job to work away from the office
- __ My willingness and ability to work independent of direct supervision
- __ A home workspace that is conducive to productivity
- __ No direct responsibilities for child/adult care during working hours
- __ My ability to separate home and family life
- __ My ability to recognize and prevent overwork

	__ Possessing the equipment, services, and support to perform my work tasks __ Other trait ________________ __ Other trait ________________
Actions I have taken to assure my telecommuting success include	
	__ Completing my company's telecommuting training course if provided and learning telecommuting policy and procedures __ Establishing a professional, organized, safe, secure, productive remote workspace __ Establishing an effective plan for quality, consistent communication __ Establishing a main office contact who will keep me informed of important activities and announcements while I am away from the main office __ Acquiring, installing, and knowing how to operate technology tools needed for effective remote work __ Having a clear telecommuting purpose and detailed remote work plan __ Other action ________________ __ Other action ________________

Once you have completed the activities outlined in this chapter, you will have fully characterized your telecommuting persona with a clear, concise description, an important step in elevating your remote work activity to the level of power telecommuter.

"True telecommuting jobs are not the norm. In fact, only four percent of telecommuting jobs are full-time, according to an October 1999 study by Human Resource Executive. *Most telecommuting jobs are hybrid positions that require contact with the workplace in a variety of locations."*

Jeff Westover, "Telecommuting–Added Perk or Added Work," www.careermag.com

To show your manager you are serious about telecommuting, you will present your telecommuter type, your attributes, your accomplishments, and your telecommuting pledge. (You will find the pledge at the end of this chapter.) If your manager is a stickler for numbers, you may wish to delay your presentation until you develop some productivity improvement detail, which I discuss in the next section.

Identifying, Tracking, Measuring, and Reporting Your Work

Sometimes in this new economy, the new workplace can be a bit overwhelming for the new employee. It seems the more you accomplish, the more projects, priorities, and responsibilities you somehow accumulate. You work hard, accomplish the impossible, fulfill your commitments, and put out fires, yet you would draw a blank if someone asked, "What did you do all day?"

Imagine the reaction you would get from your boss if after working at home all day you couldn't think of anything you accomplished. It's one of the best ways to sabotage your telecommuting privilege (more appear later in the chapter). Chris Ross, a workplace strategist at Cisco Systems, sees telecommuting as a way to "add productive work space" within the organization. Telecommuting, he believes, helps each employee create the most productive work environment possible, whether in the office, on the road, or at home.

Before you develop grand plans to show how much your productivity increases when you work at home, be cautious. Article archives are littered with stories reporting from 5 percent to well over 50 percent increases in employee performance from telecommuting.

> *"Unless the employer can find some selfish reasons to use telecommuting, I don't really care how it might help the employees or the environment. I don't think employers base their decisions about new methods on whether or not employees or regulators will like it. Instead, they are applying some very simple tests: can the new method help us reduce expenses, increase revenues, do more with less, compete better, or improve quality?"*
>
> Gil Gordon, Gil Gordon Associates

A question I hear repeatedly is "How do you know productivity has actually increased?" This is a logical question because very few organizations do a decent job of measuring the performance of knowledge workers anyway, telecommuting or not! So, when employers send people home to work, it's a stretch to think that managers have suddenly acquired new insights on employee performance measurement.

All too often these increases are the result of increased work hours, fewer interruptions, and a gut feeling that an individual has been more productive at home. Other performance increases occur because telecommuting forces managers to set worker expectations and review work that was done at home, often giving the impression that more work is being done because the manager simply knows about it. This is not to say that there was a true increase in productivity—there probably was. It is important, however, that productivity changes as a result of telecommuting be presented for what they are.

To know your telecommuting productivity improvement, you need to identify specific work tasks that you will do remotely, establish a work output baseline of the work tasks when performed in the main office, track the results of your remote work activity, show how the results differ, and then report the results to your manager.

Identifying Mobile Work Tasks

In the industrial age, in the factories as well as in the offices, it was fairly easy to quantify worker output. Processing an insurance claim or an invoice, for instance, required certain steps that were performed by several different people. Each step took a certain amount of time and had to be completed before the next step began.

In today's work environment, work activities are becoming more difficult to quantify and tend to be more reactive in nature. In an information-age office, technology allows one person to process those same claims or invoices, but this person has additional responsibility for functions such as dispute resolution, claims adjustments, account reconciliation, and other tasks that require critical thinking and functional knowledge.

No matter how complex and nonlinear information-age work may have become, though, you can break down nearly all jobs into work tasks. If you've never done this exercise for your job before, this first step can be fairly painful. But it is a must for measuring your performance.

Certain work tasks are suitable for telecommuting. Using the following form, list as many mobile work tasks as you can, showing the average time required for completion of each task while in the main office. Then, indicate what you believe are the benefits to performing each task in your remote location.

Mobile Work Task Identification Form		
Mobile Work Tasks When Performed in the Main Office	**Average Time Required in Hours**	**Benefits of Performing These Tasks in a Remote Location**

Tracking Your Work

Once you have identified typical mobile work tasks, you will need a way to track them at home. Use the "Weekly Telecommuter Task and Activity Form" on the next page to record the time it takes to perform a particular remote task. This form also allows you to track common activities such as the total number of remote work hours, phone calls, times you checked for e-mail, and so on. If you are not yet telecommuting, keep this form in mind for future use.

Weekly Telecommuter Task and Activity Form							
Performance Tasks (from your Mobile Work Task Identification Form)	**Date**	**Date**	**Date**	**Date**	**Date**	**Date**	**Date**
	Time (Hours)	**Time** (Hours)	**Time** (Hours)	**Time** (Hours)	**Time** (Hours)	**Time** (Hours)	**Time** (Hours)
Task							
Task							
Task							
Task							
Task							
Task							
Total hours worked in remote office (not including travel time)							
Miscellaneous Activities							
Number of incoming telephone calls							
Number of outgoing telephone calls							
Number of incoming e-mails							
Number of outgoing e-mails							
Number of times the dial-up line to the network was busy							
Longest wait for computer connection (minutes)							
Number of times I accessed the computer							
Number of times I accessed voice mail							
Number of times I accessed e-mail							
Other tracked activity ____________							
Other tracked activity ____________							

Quantifying Your Work

Using the two preceding forms, you will accumulate a significant amount of information for quantifying the time required for your workday activities. After four to six weeks of activity, you should see some patterns, plus you will have enough data to spot work task trends and other information useful to you and your manager. To do a thorough job of evaluating any performance changes while telecommuting, compare the data between the two forms.

Reporting Your Work

The information you gather on the Weekly Telecommuter Task and Activity Form and any analysis of work task activity can be summarized in a report you write to management. To supplement that information, here is a form that allows you to track remote work activity for the month.

Monthly Remote Work Activity Form				
Monday	**Tuesday**	**Wednesday**	**Thursday**	**Friday**
Week Beginning _______________, 20___				
Morning				
Afternoon				

Week Beginning ____________, 20___				
		Morning		
		Afternoon		
Week Beginning ____________, 20___				
		Morning		
		Afternoon		
Week Beginning ____________, 20___				
		Morning		

(continues)

(continued)

Monthly Remote Work Activity Form				
Monday	**Tuesday**	**Wednesday**	**Thursday**	**Friday**
Afternoon				

As you can see, with the proper tools, it may not be difficult to identify, quantify, track, and report your remote work activity. With these tools, you will be much better positioned to determine your telecommuting productivity improvement. Even with the best tools, however, you can still sabotage your privilege to telecommute.

The 10 Best Ways to Sabotage Your Telecommute Privilege

A comment you will hear over and over from telecommuting consultants is "Telecommuting is not for everyone." In my experience, I find this to be true. Certain people need to interact with coworkers, and others stay motivated because they know someone is watching. Others need a complete separation of work and home life, and still others have home environments not suitable for telecommuting.

Some people's perspective on acceptable behavior disqualifies them from telecommuting. A well-known executive in town explained to me that employees are generally not trustworthy and that telecommuting will never work. When I saw headlines claiming he had been moonlighting in another city on company time, I realized he wouldn't be a good candidate for telecommuting.

The point is, if you earn the privilege to telecommute, it's not an automatic and permanent condition. There are many ways to sabotage this privilege, such as the following.

1. **Lose your manager's trust:** Get caught at the golf course, at the mall, or at your kid's soccer game when you are supposed to be working, and your manager will always doubt your truthfulness. Trust is the single most valuable element you have between you and your manager. Don't lose it.
2. **Make light of your telecommuting day:** There will always be telecommuting skeptics, so joking about watching Oprah, going shopping, or even wearing bunny slippers during business hours is a sure way to stoke their fire of doubt. The power telecommuter never makes light of telecommuting. The home office should be depicted as a highly professional extension of the main office workplace.
3. **Brag about how great telecommuting is:** As long as there are people who want to work at home but for some reason cannot, there will always be telecommuting objectors. Many of these folks are prone to find any fault with remote work and capitalize on it at your expense. As an efficient workplace alternative, telecommuting should become as natural as occasional business travel.
4. **Take advantage of the privilege:** If while telecommuting you set a pattern of disappearing on Friday afternoons, taking care of the kids, or taking extra-long lunches, you may be setting yourself up for a fall. Flexibility is a byproduct of telecommuting, but work productivity should remain a primary result of the privilege.
5. **Act as if the privilege can never be taken away:** Becoming cocky as a telecommuter can cause you to take unnecessary risks. Remember that the privilege is fragile, vulnerable to the slip of the tongue, an innocent indiscretion, or a new manager.
6. **Lose your professionalism:** Loud music, missed deadlines, sloppy work, and delayed voice-mail responses are a sure way to cause manager concern. The privilege is kept by good workers who are even better as telecommuters.
7. **Return to the office on Wednesday with a complete makeover:** Changes in your appearance can send the wrong message to co-workers and management without saying a word.
8. **Disappear from the face of the virtual Earth:** Recurring unsuccessful call attempts add up quickly, leaving time for callers to imagine what you must be doing instead of work. The power telecommuter

establishes core availability hours during which callers can typically get through. When you desire quiet time, create an appropriate voice-mail message that will set expectations for returned calls. A "reach me in an emergency" instruction is good to offer just in case.

9. **Be fully versed at discussing Oprah's book of the week:** Any evidence that you were doing something during business hours other than working can be fatal to a telecommuter. As long as you use your telecommuting time wisely and discuss your nonwork activities with discretion, your professional telecommuting image will remain intact.
10. **Telecommute only on Mondays and Fridays:** A common joke about telecommuting is that "Once he starts telecommuting, we'll never see (insert your name here) on a Friday again!" One of the quickest ways to sabotage your telecommuting privilege is to have coworkers believe they're seeing a pattern of three-day weekends. If you telecommute on random days to accomplish specific tasks or complete projects, the potential for you to be the subject of this joke will be minimized.

Remember that it can take months or even years to position yourself with telecommuting credibility and a moment of indiscretion to take it away. Telecommuting is something that is continually earned, and no one said it was going to be easy. With this in mind, this is the perfect time to identify and avoid some of the most common telecommuting traps.

Avoiding the Top 10 Telecommuting Traps

As a power telecommuter, you strive to have it all together. Even in the best situations, however, the complex dynamics of the home office mixed with human emotions, family priorities, conflicting pressures from management, personality conflicts, technology incompatibilities, loads of distractions, and challenges outside your control make it impossible to keep it all together.

Working at home is natural for some and nearly impossible for others. Pat McKeown, head of the University of Georgia information systems department, calls mixing home and work life the "homogenization of time." Some people do it well, and others need clearer boundaries. No matter what name you give it, balancing work and home activities as a telecommuter can be a challenge, requiring disciplined focus, personal self-control, effective time and priority management skills, and plenty of cooperation. Do you recognize yourself in the following telecommuters who have fallen prey to the top 10 traps?

1. **Do-It-All Derrick/Daria:** Technology has empowered individuals to do the work of many. There are those (like me, for instance) who believe that if it can be done, why not do it myself? The problem with this philosophy, though, is that Do-It-All Derrick/Daria tends to take on more than can be accomplished in a day, and work tends to be completed with mediocre results. Attempting to do too many things at once breeds sloppiness and stress. To avoid the do-it-all trap, prioritize your daily duties, organize your time to focus on a single work task at a time, and delegate noncore, mundane tasks to others.
2. **Sloppy Scott/Suzi:** A disorganized home office is not only inefficient, but it can become unsafe, unsecure, and unsanitary. To show a serious commitment to telecommuting, Sloppy Scott/Suzi should clean up the primary office environment before establishing a remote office. Then, when ready to telecommute, Scott/Suzi would make the commitment from the beginning to keep an organized home office.
3. **Neighbor Ned/Nellie:** Some people love to be around others. Good neighbor Ned/Nellie will be glad to let the repairman in, sign for a package, or walk the dog for the neighbors. The way to avoid this trap is to "just say no." Explain that during work hours you are at work and cannot be interrupted except in emergencies. If you are susceptible to the good neighbor trap, either keep your telecommuting a secret from the neighbors (keep your car in the garage) or give up telecommuting.

"Workers say the ability to balance work and family is more important than any other job factor including job security, quality of working environment, and relationships with coworkers and supervisors."

Work Trends survey by the John J. Heldrich Center for Workforce Development and the Center for Survey Research and Analysis, University of Connecticut

---

4. **Multimedia Mike/Melissa:** Technology tools can increase productivity as long as the use of the tools doesn't become a project in itself. Multimedia Mike/Melissa all too often prefer to search for, add, and play with digital bells and whistles on their presentations and projects, which frequently distract them from the project's goal. This trap can be overcome by agreeing to ambitious telecommuting day work goals with your manager, leaving little time to go off on a tangent.
5. **Fix-it Frank/Fran:** Everyone likes to have these folks around whenever there's a network or software problem. Fix-it Frank/Fran enjoy a good challenge and will sometimes work hours to fix it. Although working at home makes it more difficult to get to them, they are even more tempted to "fix it" with no manager to check on them. Much like the previous trap, this can also be overcome by making ambitious telecommuting day work goals and keeping them.
6. **Scattered Steve/Sylvia:** Very often, even good workers need constant reminders of what's important to work on to meet work priorities. Sometimes these people, like Scattered Steve/Sylvia, aren't aware of how important internal cues from coworkers and the boss really are until they are gone. To avoid the scattered trap, be sure to discuss with your boss the exact work tasks you will complete each time you telecommute. This way you will fully understand the work expectations and deliver them on your return to the office.
7. **Gadget Gregg/Gilda:** These people prove that technology can increase telecommuting effectiveness but can also stifle it. Gadget Gregg/Gilda are the first in line to buy the latest palm device, wireless Internet phone, and remote-control toilet flusher (sorry Ally McBeal). These folks have motivations similar to Multimedia Mike/Melissa but use their gadgets for communication. One benefit of telecommuting is the solitude—the work time conducive to uninterrupted thought and increased work output. If anyone can call at any time and reach you anywhere, that benefit is lost. A digital pager and cell phone are excellent devices when you are on the move (as long as they are used safely). To avoid this trap is to have control over your accessibility, allowing you the option of being contacted or not.

8. **Overworked Otto/Olga:** By its very nature, telecommuting allows some of the best people to do some of their best work whenever and wherever it makes sense. In my experience, it is far more common for a telecommuter to overwork than to become a slacker, and overworking can cause a variety of problems. To avoid this trap, stick to a set of work hours except when finishing an occasional hot project. If you have trouble getting away by yourself, ask family or friends to keep you honest about your commitment by getting you away from the office.
9. **Housekeeper Harry/Harriet:** Unfinished laundry, dirty dishes, and housework a couple of steps away are too much of a temptation for Housekeeper Harry/Harriet. This kind of activity can trap even the best workers into multitasking themselves into inefficiency. Avoiding this trap takes strong will and discipline. If it gets out of hand and distracts you from your work, hold yourself to a rule that housekeeping can only be done at certain times or during breaks.

"The darkest side of the modern world seems to be that it has provided new and special kinds of hiding places for the alone, the isolated, and the depressed. Telecommuting, not to mention the rise of e-commerce on the Internet, may serve to magnify this problem manifold, as human contact is minimized and near total isolation becomes a real option rather than an oddity."

Norman Nie, professor of political science, Stanford University

10. **Secluded Sammy/Samantha:** Telecommuting to some is similar to an addictive drug: It allows freedom from common constraints; the more you do it the more you want to do it; it causes some to go off into their own world and lose track of time; and it can result in antisocial behavior. Listen carefully to others and try to live in the moment.

As you can see, you have complete control over these traps. Any of them can hold you back. When you see the slightest evidence of these pitfalls, you should spring into action and neutralize the source.

Remember, balancing work and home life as a telecommuter is a challenge that takes disciplined focus, self-control, effective time and priority management skills, and plenty of cooperation. I present tips and solutions to many of these challenges in detail later in the book. One of the best ways to assure that you stay in control of your telecommuting destiny is to make your telecommuter pledge.

Making and Solidifying Your Telecommuter Pledge

I've explained that being a telecommuter takes a special type of person and considerable work and dedication, including the following commitments stated in this chapter's opening paragraph: You fully accept telecommuting's upside and downside; you develop a work mode that meets your manager's approval; you clearly brand your telecommuter type and profile; you create obvious value in your work output; you shun self-destructive behavior; you hurdle obstacles with finesse; you avoid the traps; and you keep work in its proper perspective. In committing to all this, you make the telecommuter pledge. Many elements in the pledge are discussed throughout the book.

Making the Telecommuter Pledge	
Telecommuter Pledge and Willingness to Continue Telecommuting (check the ones that apply to you)	
As a power telecommuter, I pledge	
	__ To learn and follow my organization's telecommuting policy and procedures __ To learn and follow the organizational rules that govern equipment ownership and payment for services __ To separate work from home and family life __ To recognize and prevent overwork and excessive seclusion __ To operate as a team player and keep my work and project commitments __ To continue to effectively manage my time to the benefit of the organization

	__ To maintain an orderly, organized, safe, secure, and productive remote office __ To maintain effective communications with coworkers, management, and customers __ To track my telecommuting activity, work output, and expenses as required by management __ To always represent my telecommuting activity professionally and seriously __ To never take advantage of my telecommuting privilege and realize that this privilege may be taken away at any time __ Additional pledge: ____________________ ____________________ __ Additional pledge: ____________________ ____________________
To show my commitment to continue telecommuting, I	
	__ Would be able to convince a new manager to allow me to telecommute __ Am prepared to manage my telecommuting activities in an efficient, professional manner __ Am prepared to sign a telecommuter agreement with my company that sets the terms of my telecommuting activity __ Additional commitment: ____________________ ____________________ __ Additional commitment: ____________________ ____________________

Posturing the Pledge

Once you have identified your pledge items, transcribe them into a word-processed document and print it out. Read it and edit it until you are comfortable with it. Does it look overwhelming? Is it too much to take on? It shouldn't be. As a power telecommuter, most of these commitments should be routine.

The next logical step is to present your telecommuting pledge to your manager, right? Before you do, find out what is important to your boss. Schedule a private meeting or lunch with your boss and ask, "What would you like to see me do to assure I am as productive a telecommuter as I can be?"

Listen carefully and write down the answers. Your manager will provide you with clues about priorities and the issues that are less important. You can then make the priorities part of your pledge.

Solidifying the Pledge

Your telecommuting pledge is a commitment to quality, consistent, and professional remote work and will only have value if it is dutifully followed and regularly renewed. Once it's completed and delivered, you must abide by it. For the first three months or so, you may want to review the pledge and make a mental note about what areas may need improvement. Once these actions and changes become habit, being a power telecommuter will become routine. After that, you'll want to review and update your telecommuting pledge once each year, ideally at the same time as your employee review.

As I wrote at the chapter's start, establishing yourself as a power telecommuter is the bedrock for everything you do as a telecommuter. The devil, as they say, is in the details. The rest of this book provides you with tips and tools for developing, operating, growing, and prospering as a power telecommuter.

Chapter 3

Maximizing Contemporary Technology Tools

KEY CHAPTER POINTS

- Knowing the technology "rules" should keep you out of trouble.
- Effective remote technology boils down to knowing your platforms, potential bottlenecks, needs, and options.
- You can become technology proficient without becoming a technology geek.
- What vendors won't tell you.
- Your technology dependency may need a reality check.
- 10 ways to avoid technology gaps and disasters.
- Some rules of thumb on who pays for technology tools.
- Maximizing your present and future technology investment.

A Few "Rules" You Should Know About Technology

Technology is here to stay and will continue to make dramatic changes in our lives. As a power telecommuter, what is important for you to know about the technology you are using? How can you avoid buying technology that will soon become obsolete? How much technology should you have as backup in case your primary equipment or service fails? How do you equip your home office without breaking the bank? How can you best prepare for the next generation of technology? I answer these questions in this chapter.

Before getting too deep into telecommuting technology, I'd like to make you aware of the technology "rules":

- The Internet is allowing real-time transactions and information to be available at any time, changing the way business is being done.
- Whatever technology you are using today, it will be different very soon.
- Your technology dependency will continue to expand, and failures will continue to occur.
- You can always find someone to fix a problem and provide a service for free or dirt cheap, but you usually get what you pay for.
- The way you access the Internet and use the telephone will be very different in 10 years.
- The further you fall behind in technology, the harder it is to catch up.

If you keep these "rules" in mind as you make your telecommuting technology decisions, you will tend to remain aware of technology challenges, ask the right questions, and stay out of real trouble.

A Telecommuter's Technology Primer

Technology can be confusing, not only because it is complex but also because it changes so quickly. Between the time this text was written and the moment you read it, some products and services have advanced into the next generation. Others have become obsolete. How can you keep up? How can you confidently invest in a technology platform (Mac versus PC, Microsoft Office versus Corel WordPerfect Office, Palm Handheld versus Pocket PC, and so on) not knowing if it will be compatible with your employer and the rest of the world next year?

Should you only use products and services provided by your employer, or should you make an investment on your own? What should you do when your computer or other tool has technical problems? Which technology tools can make your job easier and help you stay in the loop with customers, coworkers, and the boss?

To answer these and other critical technology-related questions, you will need to know what main office technology platforms are being used, what accessibility options are available to you (dial-up modem versus options with acronyms like DSL and ISDN, for instance), and the location of your remote-capacity bottlenecks. Only then can you begin selecting your computing options, your telecommunication options, your service and support options, and your accessibility options.

Remember, Today's Technology Is Still Quite Volatile

Many people, including me, have a love/hate relationship with computers. A computer can be a highly productive tool when it does what it's supposed to do. When it doesn't, I've often been tempted to throw mine out the window (pun intended!).

Even though, as Bill Gates predicted over 10 years ago, nearly every desk has a computer, and even though the bulk of all computing is being done on Windows-based PCs, and even though applications providers have had over 10 years to get it right, computers are not all that stable. The next time you commit an "illegal operation" or cause a "fatal error," remember that this technology is quite immature.

"This is the first time in the history of the world that consumers are willing to pay for instruments that don't work," said author Peter F. Drucker in his keynote presentation at the 2000 LOMA Systems Forum in San Diego, California, on April 25, 2000. "There is nothing in all of history that is as badly engineered and works as poorly as a computer."

(continues)

(continued)

Every time your computer locks up, you may be witnessing evidence of a rapidly changing, highly complicated technology being introduced so fast that many bugs of previous generations are packaged with it. In their haste to get products to market, even the best suppliers create goods that don't always work without trouble. Experts have advised me to shy away from the first generation of any product until it has stabilized. Add to that the learning curve for both the consumer and the supplier that comes with any major change, and technology can become costly for everyone involved.

As troublesome as today's technology sometimes seems to be, access to the information superhighway is critical to the contemporary worker. This chapter will help you make the best choices.

What Main Office Technology Platforms Are Being Used?

The employer usually dictates a telecommuter's technology platform. To minimize incompatibilities, wasted energy, and time converting files; to stay in the loop; and to work as if you're one cubicle away, do whatever you can to use the same platforms at the same release level as your employer for the following items. While you may not use or need all of this technology, this list provides a good point of reference.

- **Common software applications:** Word processor, calendar, e-mail, contact manager, portable devices, and Web browser.
- **Network access:** Dial-up, computer-to-computer, computer-to-network, virtual private network, and Intranet/Internet.
- **Security:** Compatibility, common encryption, privacy control, and password assignment.
- **Transmission/Connectivity:** Analog, integrated services digital network (ISDN), advanced digital subscriber loop (ADSL), Internet protocol (IP) networks, computer telephony integration (CTI), frame relay, cable modem, digital satellite, wireless, and personal communications system (PCS).

- **Activity tracking:** Systems that track calls, e-mail, work tasks, and projects.
- **Accessibility and efficiency applications:** Smart search, computer-based telephony, message paging, personal digital assistants (PDAs), groupware, group calendaring, and always-on Internet.

Your primary goal in choosing platforms is to assure connectivity with the main office to prevent from becoming an island. Using the organization's platforms of choice for telecommuting, even if they are not the ideal for you, assures *connectivity* because you use the same technology, *support* because technical staff is familiar with the technology you are using, and *budget* from the organization because the technology is approved for use.

"Technology does not drive telecommuting—it enables it."
Eddie Caine, professional services manager for TManage

Now that I have recommended that you stick with your employer's technology platform, let me toss out another rule of thumb: As the technology continuum moves forward, compatibility issues tend to go away. Today, for instance, the Internet and conversion software allow incompatibility problems with e-mail systems, computer platforms, and many software applications to all but disappear. Therefore, as time goes on, it is more likely that you can use equipment and services independent of existing organizational platforms. It is up to you to research compatibility issues each time you make a decision to use a specific technology tool.

At this point you might be saying, "This is way too complicated. I can't deal with all this stuff!" or "Who's supposed to pay for all this?" If this looks overly complicated, it really isn't. Later in this chapter you will see how the choices are very logical and broken down into bite-sized chunks based on information you already have. In a later section, I also talk about who usually pays for technology. Next, however, you need to begin identifying and monitoring your remote-capacity bottlenecks.

Where Are Your Remote-Capacity Bottlenecks?

As the pace of technological change increases, capacity bottlenecks are likely to pop up more frequently. Each time you satisfy one bottleneck, another seems to emerge. At least you can be assured that with the proper advice, correct tools, and some cash, you can overcome just about any capacity bottleneck. What kinds of bottlenecks am I talking about? Here's a review.

- **Storage:** Do you have (and need) the capacity to store and back up large documents, audio and video files, and databases? To store paper documents? To back up your operating system and computer configuration?
- **Transmission:** Does your telephone/data transmission service allow you to send and receive files, Web pages, and multimedia with reasonable speed? Is the main office transmission medium available from your local provider? Do you have an alternate telephone/data transmission service provider? (A cell phone would be a critical lifeline if a backhoe cut the cable in your neighborhood.)
- **ISP:** Does your Internet service provider (ISP) have limitations on attachment file size or transmission speeds? Is its network reliable? Are you signed up with an alternate ISP? If service to your primary ISP went out, a secondary service would keep you in communication.
- **Processing:** Will your computer processor meet your increasing demands? Do you anticipate that your processing demands will increase due to access to large graphic, audio, or video files, video conferencing, or Web streaming?

"In today's world of changing technology, the rule of thumb is whatever capacity you have today, it's not enough."

Michael Dziak

- **Conversion:** Are you able to use work documents on your home computer? Are you able to scan paper documents? Are you capable of converting and reading nonstandard application formats?

- **RAM:** Insufficient random access memory (RAM) slows your computer response time considerably. How much is installed on your computer? To determine the RAM installed on your Windows 95 or 98 machine, click on "Start, Settings, Control Panel, System, and General." This page shows your processor type and the currently installed RAM. Many programs recommend a minimum 24MB to run. I recommend having a minimum of 120MB if your computer can handle it. Consult the instruction manual for your computer motherboard to determine its RAM capacity and RAM chip type.
- **Multiplicity:** Are you able to receive an e-mail and fax simultaneously? Can you be talking with technical support while troubleshooting a problem online? (You should have at least one extra business line, ideally two.) Technologies like ISDN and ADSL provide simultaneous voice and data, but if one's down, they're likely both going to be down.

Why is it so important that telecommuters overcome technology bottlenecks? First, you can pretty much expect bottlenecks to raise their ugly head and stop you from working when you are on deadline or running late for a meeting. Second, with the speed of technology changes, bottlenecks are bound to happen. If you anticipate and plan for them as you make technology investments, your purchase decisions will remain much more informed.

Selecting Your Basic Technology Options

What kind of technology will you need for effective remote work? Before that question can be answered, you must first determine the work tasks you will be performing. As stated earlier, a rule of thumb for selecting telecommuting technology is to have access to at least the same technology tools and performance available in the main office for the tasks selected for remote work. Once you identify your needs, work with technical staff on issues involving adequate incoming ports at the main office, data speeds, connectivity type, access instructions, security protocols, availability of telephone service to your home, and so on. Here are some specifics.

Consider Your Computing Options

Decisions, decisions. PC or Mac? Palm Handheld or Pocket PC? The bottom line is this: The tasks you plan to do and where you plan to do them will determine computing and communications power and type. Some tasks, such as technical reading, proofreading, brainstorming, updating employee evaluations, or sorting through an overflowing in-box after vacation may require no computing power at all.

> *"Civilization advances by extending the number of important operations which we can perform without thinking."*
> Alfred North Whitehead, English mathematician and philosopher (1861–1947)

A product manager or trainer who occasionally works at home may need just a word processor and a modem to check e-mail messages. A technical support engineer for a software company may need a high-capacity workstation, CD-ROM reader, and high-speed digital connections. For ideas and advice on the ideal computing equipment for the work you do, tap into the technical resources available through your employer and use Table 3.2 later in the chapter for some guidance on selecting remote-technology tools.

Consider Your Telecommunication Options

Selecting telecommunication options can be confusing, especially for non-technical telecommuters. Here are a few rules of thumb for your consideration.

- **Add a separate telecommuting telephone line for phone calls even if you have to pay for it yourself:** This will separate personal calls from business calls. Include some basic features such as call-waiting, conferencing, and call-forwarding, plus some type of answering device with remote access. These features are common to a business environment and can be vital for staying in the loop.
- **Add a separate data and fax line if you expect high usage or need incoming fax availability:** Most telephone companies offer a service that provides a separate telephone number but operates over an existing line. An incoming fax will have a distinctive ring that can be recognized by an inexpensive switch, automatically routing fax calls to a fax machine or modem.

- **For dial-up applications, choose the fastest modem you can find (probably 56 Kbps):** Digital communication—ISDN, T1, frame relay, asynchronous transfer mode (ATM)—is becoming more available and is beneficial when large data files, graphics, or video are regularly transmitted, or when Web speed is important. Price and availability of these services vary. Consult with your information services experts to discuss the pros and cons, availability, limitations, benefits, costs, and their preference.
- **Select data speeds that give you at least the same response you have in the office:** When using your computer, the delay on the screen when moving from one page to another or after clicking on a toolbar can be frustrating. It is called *screen refresh delay* and can occur for a variety of reasons. In selecting data communication speeds, strive to have your computer screen refresh time the same as or better than your remote location.

How critical is your need for speed? Today you may only need to send and receive relatively small Word files and download an occasional program. Using a dial-up connection may be adequate. As you send and receive more and more bandwidth-hungry multimedia (things like audio clips, videoconferencing, video, animation, and Internet telephone), your tolerance for download time will wear thin. Only you know where that tolerance level is, and once you reach it, it's time to upgrade your data speed. Here are approximate transmission times for sending files of various size, according to Dean Brown, president of Star Valley Communications, a communications consulting and marketing firm specializing in remote work.

Table 3.1. Comparing the Speeds of Sending Common Applications

	Dial-up (56 Kbps)	ISDN (128 Kbps)	ADSL (1.5 Mbps)	Cable Modem (4.0 Mbps)
250K word-processed document	35 seconds	17 seconds	1.3 seconds	0.5 seconds
2MB picture	4.5 minutes	2.4 minutes	10.7 seconds	4 seconds
9MB video clip	25 minutes	10 minutes	48 seconds	18 seconds

Consider Equipment Service and Support Options

Equipment service and support decisions should be made based on your telecommuting frequency, the requirements and nature of your work tasks, your budget, and a variety of other factors. No matter who is responsible for equipment, service, and support, the following questions must be considered:

- Who will you contact to troubleshoot problems?
- How will software and hardware be updated?
- Is the company software licensed to be installed on your personal computer?
- Who will order telephone service and where should the bill be sent?
- How will you keep track of your equipment, upgrades, and service activity?
- Where will equipment go when it's no longer needed?
- How do you order new equipment when you need it?

Because a simple modem failure or a software glitch can render you out of service, smart telecommuters address these and other equipment service and support issues before telecommuting begins. Although a thorough telecommuting policy and agreement with your employer should cover most of these questions, it remains your responsibility to prevent technology-related work interruptions. You will find some tips, ideas, and suggestions later in this chapter.

Consider Your Accessibility Options

All the technology in the world is meaningless to you without consistent accessibility. As a telecommuter, you must identify the locations from which you will need access (home office, airports, hotel rooms, customer locations), and then determine the type of connection (Internet, dial-up, wireless) and capacity (transmission speeds, multiplicity, and so on). Once you determine your needs, you will be able to develop a plan that consistently meets them.

How do you develop your plan? The best way to start is to make a simple list of your access needs based on location. The following worksheet should help you identify your communication needs. The first section is filled in as a sample.

Sample

Communication Needs Assessment Worksheet

Work Location	Communications Application	What I Have Access to Now	What I Need
Home	Voice telephone calls	Standard phone line	Cellular as a backup
	E-mail/Fax/Internet access with desktop computer	Second phone line	—
	E-mail/Fax/Internet access with notebook computer	Second phone line	—
	E-mail/Fax/Internet access with personal digital assistant (PDA)	—	Wireless adapter
	Fax/Teleconference	—	Third phone line
	Product demonstrations/Videoconference (high speed)	—	High-speed access line
	Other Interactive paging	—	Interactive pager

Communication Needs Assessment Worksheet			
Work Location	**Communication Application**	**What I Have Access to Now**	**What I Need**
Home	Voice telephone calls		
	E-mail/Fax/Internet access with desktop computer		
	E-mail/Fax/Internet access with notebook computer		
	E-mail/Fax/Internet access with PDA		
	Fax/Teleconference		
	Product demonstrations/Videoconference (high speed)		
	Other ______________________ ______________________		
Airport	Voice telephone calls		
	E-mail/Fax/Internet access with notebook computer		
	E-mail/Fax/Internet access with PDA		
	Voice mail/Teleconference		
	Videoconference (high speed)		
	Other ______________________ ______________________		

Communication Needs Assessment Worksheet			
Work Location	**Communication Application**	**What I Have Access to Now**	**What I Need**
Hotel	Voice telephone calls		
	E-mail/Fax/Internet access with notebook computer		
	E-mail/Fax/Internet access with PDA		
	Voice mail/teleconference		
	Videoconference (high speed)		
	Other ____________________ ____________________		
Other location ________	Voice telephone calls		
	E-mail/Fax/Internet access with notebook computer		
	E-mail/Fax/Internet access with PDA		
	Voice mail/teleconference		
	Videoconference (high speed)		
	Other ____________________ ____________________		

Now that you have identified your needs, you have to acquire the necessary technology tools and find a way to get connected wherever you happen to be.

Equipping Your Home Office

When making equipment decisions, the first thing you need to ask is "what work will I be doing there and what do I need to complete it successfully?" Table 3.2 offers ideas on the equipment and services you should be considering based on the kind of telecommuting you will be doing.

Table 3.2. Home Office Technology Tools for Selected Remote Tasks

Position Examples	Typical Tasks Performed	Suggested Equipment and Services
Marketing staff	Reading trade press	Telephone, work materials and files, paper, writing utensils, reference materials, and other supplies
Procurement specialist	Reviewing proposals	
Accounting support	Reviewing accounting books	
Collections agent	Making collections calls	
Attorney	Editing legal documents	Everything above plus . . . business telephone line, speakerphone, cellular phone, computer equipped with software, CD-ROM drive, data backup medium, 56 Kbps modem, voice mail, mail, printer, battery backup, lightning protection, e-mail/Internet access, antivirus protection, Internet security/firewall protection
Product manager	Developing product plans	
Technical writer	Editing documents	
Auditor	Reviewing accounting records	
Public relations professional	Writing/Sending press releases	
Economist	Writing/Sending studies/articles	
Supervisor/manager	Writing employee reviews	
Copywriter/Journalist	Composing articles	Everything above plus . . . dedicated fax/modem line, high-speed telephone line, notebook computer equipped with fax software, a fax switch, CD-ROM recorder with DVD player, speakers and sound card
Architect	Developing architectural plans	
Typist/Transcriptionist	Transcribing verbal records	
Computer programmer	Writing code	
Human resources staff	Conducting interviews	
Information systems engineer	Remote technical support	
Real estate agent	Searching home listings	
Lobbyist	Accessing legislation	

Position Examples	Typical Tasks Performed	Suggested Equipment and Services
Marketing manager Project manager Sales executive Technical support	Extensive Internet research Remote project management High-end virtual office Interactive technical support	Everything above plus . . . document scanner, computer docking station, video/audio mixer
Design engineer Telemarketer Reservation agent	Remote product design Remote customer contact Airline/hotel reservations	Everything above plus . . . Internet protocol telephony, large-screen monitor, high-capacity telephone
CAD/CAM engineer Graphic artist Corporate executive	Remote drafting Remote animation Virtual office/corporation	Everything above plus . . . videoconferencing equipment, CAD/CAM graphics hardware

If this looks fairly complicated to you today, fear not. As you identify each need and acquire the equipment and services to meet those needs, it will get much simpler. Part of the comfort zone involves learning enough about technology to make it useful, but not spending so much time on the learning process that your work suffers significantly. I next talk about some ways you can do just that.

Mastering Technology Without Becoming a Technology Geek

There is no doubt that good craftspeople must have good tools, but it's the work that they get paid for, not the tools. The same applies to the power telecommuter. Sure, it's important to have a working knowledge of your operating system, of basic troubleshooting, and of maintenance, but your time spent producing the work for which you were hired is much more valuable to your employer than taking a half day to install software.

As a driven knowledge worker, you tend to be self-sufficient, typically solving problems on your own even though they are outside your expertise. There is, however, a point of diminishing returns when you tackle a project that gets beyond your capabilities. Here are some ways you can master your technology tools without becoming a technology geek.

- **Get a book for technology beginners:** The "For Dummies" books are usually well written and can be excellent resources. I became functional at designing Web pages in an afternoon with such a book. I refer to it regularly and still use the software that came with it. If it is well written, this type of book can provide an invaluable resource.
- **Make friends with someone who knows much more than you:** I'm sure you have met people who know more about spreadsheet software or fax software than you do. Keep a file of names associated with the product so that when you're stuck, you'll know who to call. Keep these people on your holiday gift list!
- **Make friends with a techie:** A good computer geek is hard to find. Since I started my business in 1991, I've always had a "digital blacksmith" available who provides me with advice on technology decisions, advises me on the best tools for what I want to accomplish, and remains on call for troubleshooting problems. A good digital blacksmith can set up your computers to run faster and help you find specialty software, networking tools, back-up devices, troubleshooting and security software, and so on. When you find one who is always looking for a challenge *and* is capable of the work, *definitely* add this person to your holiday gift list.
- **Discover the world of shareware:** How would you like to download almost-free software that could change your life? I know that this sounds like one of those spam pitches, but it is for the most part true. Shareware is legitimate software typically written by talented independent programmers (by now much of the shareware is commercialized) who couldn't find a tool to meet their needs, so they made one themselves and share it with others. The authors

allow you to use the software and, if you like it, send a reasonable fee for its use (usually allowing you access to technical support and notifications of updates). There are dozens of sites from which shareware (plus freeware and evaluation copies of software) may be downloaded. These sites have titles for business, networking, utilities, multimedia, Internet, communications, desktop tools, and many others. My favorite shareware software is Paint Shop Pro, which allows me to open, convert, and modify nearly any graphic file. See "Telecommuter Resources on the Web" in the back of the book for some shareware site listings.

- **Stay current through continuous learning:** Training on the use of voice mail, e-mail, collaborative software, and other technology tools can dramatically improve your effectiveness. Don't hesitate to register for company-sponsored training or take courses on your own. They can make your telecommuting experience that much more successful and rewarding. Continuous education in the use of technology tools is important enough that if your employer doesn't cover the cost, make the investment yourself and take a tax deduction.
- **Identify and meet your support team:** If you are fortunate enough to be supported by an information technology (IT) group, be sure to meet the individual who has responsibility for remote-access support. If you are *really* fortunate and have a team of IT experts with responsibilities broken down by function (network, operating system, applications, security, maintenance, upgrades, and so on), meet each one of them. Any one of these folks could pull you out of a jam some day, so establishing a relationship can pay off handsomely.
- **Tap into the knowledge of vendors:** Service and equipment providers for telephone service, network equipment, and communication software can be an excellent resource for making technology decisions. You can learn a whole lot about platforms and applications, plus get free coffee and bagels, at the free product seminars that are going on all the time (see listings in your local paper or on vendor Web pages). Vendors with good marketing departments will have case studies and testimonials to which the average user can relate.

As you can see, you can keep up with technology without dedicating your life to it. You simply need to establish technology learning, acquisitions, and relationships as a priority. How do you do this without becoming a technology geek? As a power telecommuter, you should ideally have

- A good working knowledge of the technology tools you are using, allowing you maximize your daily work productivity
- Reasonable replacement options available in case of some kind of failure to reduce downtime
- Access to technical support for troubleshooting, recovery assistance, and technology replacement

As a part of that knowledge, it is important to stay aware of how the vendor world operates so that you are better prepared to make informed decisions on purchases.

Some Things Equipment and Service Vendors Won't Tell You

Being a vendor in today's market must be a challenge. As we entered the year 2000, e-commerce and dot-com business models were peaking in a frenzy of initial public offering excitement, carrying the stock market to an all-time high. But in the summer of 2000, as profits appeared to be elusive and the dot-com novelty wore off, the market fell hard.

By the very nature of today's market environment, the life cycle of a typical technology product is not measured in years, but in months. The wrong decision in any product development stage can be disastrous, causing what otherwise may be an excellent product to miss its market opportunity, then crash and burn. These market conditions have spawned some clever ways for vendors to supplement their sales income. Here are some points that vendors won't go out of their way to tell you.

- **The old "cheap razor, expensive blades" trick is back:** Nearly 100 years ago, razor manufacturers developed a brilliant marketing strategy: Give away fancy razors and then sell the blades at a high price. It seems the technique is back. I bought a reconditioned color printer from a well-known manufacturer at what I believed was an excellent price. What I didn't know was that the tiny replacement print (toner) cartridges that lasted just two to three months retailed for about a third of the hardware cost. So every six months I pay this company the equivalent of a new machine for the privilege of printing. The point is, when making purchase decisions, be sure to take into account all the operating costs, not just the initial purchase price.

- **You often get what you pay for when it's free:** The Web is full of "free" opportunities that should be studied well before making a commitment. Several Internet service providers, for instance, offer connectivity and an e-mail account at no charge. Although these services may be ideal as a backup, be cautious when considering them as your primary service. Besides the sometimes aggravating pop-up ads, these services have been known to be overloaded and unavailable during peak times. And, because the e-mail address you are issued is exclusive to that service, if the service goes out of business (which many already have), what a pain it will be to notify all your contacts that your address has changed. Also, as a power telecommuter, you should decide if an e-mail address with known free ISP is the image you wish to present.
- **Updates are for them, not for you:** Although I normally take the optimistic "half full" outlook on issue discussions, experience shows that a software revision is frequently released to solve a compatibility issue or fix a problem. This is usually not a bad thing, but it's useful to know why a product is being upgraded, especially if a cost is involved. If you are upgrading critical software, you may want to read the notes included so there won't be any surprises. And, as mentioned previously, when using the same software as your employer, it is preferable to use the same revision level.
- **Long-term contracts are not necessarily required:** For most products and services, competition has forced long-term contracts to become fairly obsolete. Getting stuck with a two-year cellular phone contract can be very painful when you hear that a competitor offers the same service but with free long distance. No matter what service you are buying, shop around for the best deal and for the shortest contract time.

"The Research Center at the University of Georgia found that in metro Atlanta, more households have cell phones than pets."
Jeffry Scott, "Near and Dear Are Our Pets," *Atlanta Journal-Constitution*, June 6, 1999

- **Costs are hidden in the fine print:** Competition has driven monthly charges for popular services such as cell phones so low that your dealer may attempt to recover some costs in the fine print. I recently upgraded my cellular service and through the process was surprised (and pretty angry) at the hidden costs and service charges that reduced the transaction's value. There was a $20 per line processing fee, a $30 per phone equipment change fee, and $10 for a charger. Watch for these fees, and if you are unable to negotiate them down, you may want to take your business elsewhere.
- **If there's a back door, someone will find it:** No matter how secure you believe your systems and software to be, it is wise to have a healthy skepticism of their infallibility. To be convinced, monitor a computer security alert service for a couple of months and you will discover the vulnerabilities of "secure" systems on the market. One such service provides notifications from the Computer Emergency Response Team (CERT) Coordination Center at no charge. See www.cert.org.
- **If one of the bells breaks, the whistles may go with it:** As technology products physically become smaller, engineers are combining previously separate functions into single items. For example, you can buy a combined telephone and answering machine, a computer motherboard with a built-in modem, and a computer and monitor all-in-one unit. This is really good for consumer prices, but really bad if one part of the system stops working. If one function fails, you've lost everything while the whole unit is being repaired. When you have no choice but to buy combination products, be prepared to have a back-up plan for the main components in case a function goes bad.
- **Once you go down that path, you may be stuck with the destination:** Think of your software as a tool to accept, format, store, organize, sort, display, and distribute information. Your business

accounting or e-mail program, for instance, accepts your typing and formats your text as data, allowing you to store, organize, and sort the information among other data. It then allows you to see the information you have created and print it or send it to someone else. If you decide to change business accounting or e-mail software, will you be able to transfer and use the data without having to retype everything? Data transferability should be a part of your purchase decision.

There are diminishing returns to spending hours researching technology purchases. You have heard this before, but it's especially valid when dealing with technology that keeps you in the loop: If it sounds too good to be true, it probably is.

Take the time to know what you need, research the market for the best solution, negotiate the best deal, and get back to work. Many excellent resources are available online to help you make an informed decision on products and services (see the resources section at the end of this book). As technology becomes a bigger part of your life, you will need to occasionally do a reality check and make sure you are positioned to prevent gaps and disasters.

Your Technology Dependency May Need a Reality Check

Think for a moment how much you are not dependent on technology during any part of the day. Transaction automation and information access has no doubt made certain elements of our lives more convenient.

"An explosion in Internet use is driving the change. More than 14 million Web sites are registered, with 59 percent of them based in the USA. But with the rest of the world discovering cyberspace, industry experts estimate by 2003, the Internet will be populated by 160 million registered sites, most of them overseas."

Marilyn Geewax, "Rapid Growth Sparks Fight for Internet Control," *Atlanta Journal-Constitution*, July 24, 2000

Trust is the cornerstone of the entire system. We trust that that electronic transaction is available, that it completes the transaction accurately, that our personal information is kept confidential, and that our transactions are secure against fraud and personal profiling. We trust that the car will start, that the cellular system will connect our calls, that an important e-mail will arrive with its attachments, that our money will be available from the automated teller machine, and that our personal and business information is protected.

As you become more dependent on technology as a critical element of your personal and professional life, how trusting should you be? As a power telecommuter, how vulnerable are you to telephone cable cuts, network computer glitches, lightning storms, hackers, viruses, credit card fraud, a lost or stolen notebook or PDA, excessive junk e-mail, and plain old equipment failures? Even if using the most popular software and service providers, you should have cause for concern. Consider these headlines from news sources on information breaches alone:

- (Large software manufacturer) slammed for e-mail security holes
- (Popular Web browser) hole exposes Web surfers' private data
- (Popular browser supplier) tests patches for security hole
- (Large software manufacturer's) browser bug may access private files
- (Popular free e-mail service) users missing old e-mail, address books
- E-mail addresses broadcast by big companies
- The devil you don't know: Strange banks are selling your private information, too
- (Large microprocessor manufacturer) grapples with security glitch in server
- (Internet bank) security breach could affect other banks

To presume your personal information and private e-mail are private can be quite naive. Are you protecting yourself against these and other vulnerabilities? What would you do if your e-mail, Internet access, or telephone services were down for two days? How would you recover from a hard disk failure, a catastrophic virus, or a burglary of your home? This subject begs a whole separate book to explore properly, but you can do a few simple things to reduce vulnerability.

10 Ways to Prevent Technology Gaps and Disasters

Suppose you have about three hours of work left on a key presentation for an upcoming sales meeting. You promised your manager you would e-mail the information by 3 p.m. today, and you can't afford to be late. It's 7 a.m., and when you try to open the document, your word processor announces: "Your program has performed an illegal action. If you continue, all information will be deleted."

You try all the usual fixes like rebooting, using scan disk, and even reloading the word processor, and it still doesn't work. By now it's 9 a.m. and you're beginning to panic. What should you do?

This scenario illustrates how vulnerable telecommuters are to failure of key technology. If you were in the office, you would simply use another computer or call IT support to come fix yours. But when you are alone at home and something goes wrong with critical equipment, it's a different story.

There are four basic elements critical to remote work: a power source, a computer, a telephone, and connectivity. As a telecommuter, what would you do if you lost any one of them? How would you convince your boss that it was a legitimate problem and not something you conveniently created to stall for more time?

The unexpected failure or loss of technology can cause significant harm to the power telecommuter, sometimes requiring days for recovery. You can prevent or lessen the effects of such situations with the following ideas.

1. **Have a plan B:** Ideally, you should have a back-up mechanism and plan for each critical element in your technology arsenal. This includes a back-up computer (complete with a duplicated hard drive with your critical data), back-up local and long-distance telephone service (consider a cell phone and prepaid long-distance

card), back-up e-mail and Internet access, and temporary power. If the Internet ever goes down, there's always the trusty old fax to use in place of e-mail. Your goal should be to experience as little down time as possible, especially if skeptics are lying in wait for evidence that telecommuting shouldn't be allowed. Here are a few more specifics.

- As finicky as computers can be, and as inexpensive as computers are today, you can probably justify having a complete second computer setup. If any one component goes out (for example: modem, monitor, keyboard, hard drive), you have an automatic alternative (assuming the two systems are compatible). I regularly find myself moving from one computer to the other, allowing me to get more done! If you network them together, you can have an automatic back-up system.
- I've kept a minimum of two, and sometimes three, separate ISPs at one time for a variety of reasons. It's not uncommon for an e-mail server to go down at the precise moment you need to send an important letter or proposal. If that happens, you simply send the e-mail from your other address, explaining it's temporary.
- Have an alternate printing option. One weekend day my printer blew out in the middle of a hot job and I was stuck. Although I'm not advocating the investment in a backup printer per se, start looking around for another alternative such as a 24-hour Kinko's or a neighbor's printer.

2. **Protect your hardware:** As technology becomes smaller and more portable, you will need to take additional precautions to protect your hardware and prevent failures. You must protect hardware from its common enemies, which include beverages, extreme heat and cold, dust, static electricity, magnets, improper storage and moving, lightning, and power surges.
3. **Protect your software:** It is critical that you protect your software and data with a firewall, antivirus software and service, and privacy control. With intrusive worms, hacker intrusion, and computer viruses becoming more common (especially when using always-on Internet services), protection against these pests is essential. Firewalls are designed to safeguard your computer from unauthorized access

while online. Privacy-control software helps you keep your private information to yourself (including protecting personal information away from unwanted intrusions from your employer) and allows you to decide if an intruding "cookie" should remain on your hard drive. Finally, you'll need regularly updated antivirus software to scan for, detect, and neutralize computer viruses. You will find an excellent resource for security options, definitions, and resources at the Information Systems Security Association (ISSA) Web page at www.issa.org. Click on "Links."

4. **Have your equipment serviced by the pros:** I recently paid nearly $600 to add 64MB of RAM to my new computer. I searched and found the best deal on the RAM chips, but while installing it I blew out the motherboard. And, since this six-month-old computer was already obsolete, I had to buy a whole new case to boot! The lesson? Unless you're willing to take the chance, a trained professional should work on anything inside the computer.
5. **Use a battery back-up system:** I used to live in the fastest growing county in the fastest growing region in the country. With all that construction and almost-daily AC power stutters and brownouts, it took just a few lost files for me to become the fastest growing advocate of battery back-up systems. I have one on each of my computers to assure steady AC, to protect from transient voltages from the AC and telephone line, and to allow me time to finish what I'm working on and shut down the computer when the power goes out during a storm. They are as simple to install as a power strip, and I paid less than $100 for each unit.
6. **Back up your computer frequently:** Notice I didn't say "back up your data." Your whole computer should be backed up onto a medium that allows immediate recovery, such as a large-capacity tape or CD. If you only backed up your data and the hard drive crashed, it might take you well into two days to reload all your programs and then go to the Web to make them all current. My digital blacksmith recommends keeping a complete duplicate of my hard drive on a second computer and then updating it regularly. If my main hard drive fails, I can replicate it by transferring the entire software set to a new hard drive in one operation instead of possibly hundreds. In addition, I keep a frequently updated copy of my

important files on tape outside the home office just in case. How frequently should you back up? It depends on the amount of work you do and how vital the information is. I recommend a total backup every 30 days at minimum.

7. **Buy more memory and hard-drive capacity than you think you'll need:** In the early nineties when I upgraded my RAM to 8MB, I thought I was in tall digital cotton. Before long, however, the old capacity rule came into play, and I had a RAM shortage. Whenever the computer is low on memory or reaching hard-drive capacity, your computer slows down and error messages become more frequent. So, when your hard drive approaches 75 percent capacity and when RAM goes on sale, it's time to upgrade.
8. **Keep software current:** Although it can sometimes be costly, keeping software up to date is important. As explained before, an update often contains fixes for anomalies found in the last revision, plus new features that make the application more useful. Besides, your technical support folks appreciate it when all employees are using the same software. Finally, updating your software assures compatibility with others using the same software when you share files.
9. **Keep your information and equipment secure:** The advantages of having megabytes of information available in a notebook or PDA are great, but so are the risks. I don't have to describe the consequences of having equipment lost, stolen, or damaged while on the road. One solution is to store vital information on the network, accessible by password when needed, and keeping the bare minimum of data on portable devices. Always keep your data and network access password-protected to minimize unwelcome penetration if your device is stolen. Finally, keep close tabs on your equipment while you are on the move. Certain people are looking for opportunities to grab your computer when you least expect it.
10. **Stay safe in the use of your technology:** Above all, your work should be done in a safe, healthy environment. Prevent unsafe conditions by keeping your work area uncluttered and orderly, never overloading electrical outlets, repairing frayed wires, keeping all wiring organized, using space heaters safely, repairing or replacing broken furniture, stacking boxes properly, using appropriate equip-

ment stands, and properly handling and disposing of hazardous materials. Install smoke detectors and a carbon monoxide detector. Have a plan for reacting to emergencies such as fires, thunderstorms, and power outages. Have a home office safety checklist, a fire extinguisher, a flashlight, a portable radio with extra batteries, an emergency numbers list, and an evacuation plan for your home office.

As you can see, many of these steps are simple, and some are free. You're probably already doing a few of them. At the risk of preaching, I feel that preventing and being prepared for technology gaps and disasters should be high on your priority list.

Who Pays for Equipment, Services, and Support?

Many managers see telecommuting as an additional expense with little or no measurable return. Others see it as a wise investment in organizational efficiency.

Some organizations provide complete service and support to their telecommuters, and others leave their telecommuters to fend for themselves. While a case can be made for an employer investing in full telecommuter support, many managers are simply not yet convinced. Therefore, you may have to take on the lion's share of support responsibility and expense yourself.

Keep in mind that if you are not willing to invest your own hard-earned money into telecommuting, you have the option of commuting to the office every day. As you face the decision to invest more deeply in your own telecommuting (and try to convince your employer to pick up some of the tab), you may wish to consider these general rules of thumb for how technology should be supported and who pays.

- **The telecommuting frequency:** Full-time telecommuters need to be supported as if they were in the main office. The less frequently you telecommute, the more likely it is that you will have to pay for equipment and services and handle problems on your own.

- **The distance from the main office:** If your employer provides support, distance usually affects only how equipment is serviced. If you live a significant distance from the main office, a case for full on-site support can be argued. If you are a local telecommuter, you can bring equipment in for service and work in the main office until the remote equipment is repaired.
- **Equipment ownership:** Whoever owns the remote equipment, including software and hardware, should pay for maintenance, upgrades, repair, and replacement. A notable alternative is illustrated by the Delta Air Lines Wired Workforce program in which employees pay a low monthly fee for three years to purchase computer equipment, gain Internet access, and 24/7 technical support.
- **The number of telecommuters:** As a company adds telecommuters, it becomes more economical to equip and support them.
- **The means of network access:** Dial-up remote access can become cost prohibitive, especially in areas where local telephone service is metered. Support from your employer should be expected if you have built a good case for telecommuting.
- **The requirements of the tasks:** The more complicated and/or bandwidth-hungry a task, the more support you need. Different tasks require different equipment. As a power telecommuter, you know your technology needs for the various tasks you perform remotely and can expect your employer to provide adequate support while telecommuting.
- **The nature of the work:** The level of dependence on electricity, a computer, a telephone, and connectivity for remote work tasks determines urgency of support. If a customer service representative loses any one element, productivity screeches to a halt. A product manager, however, can continue writing a document locally even if the network or telephone service is down. Once you are telecommuting, the more important your remote work is to meeting critical needs, the more likely the organization will cover the costs.

- **The staffing level of the IT department:** If the IT staff is overburdened, remote workers should be expected to handle problems on their own or the organization should outsource support.
- **The budget available:** Telecommuting can be done on a shoestring budget, but is not usually very efficient or highly recommended. Telecommuters may have to bear the technology, maintenance, and support expense burden temporarily while the case for remote work is being established. When the business case is proven, the employer can be expected to cover these expenses.
- **The different types of support:** There are nearly as many types of support as there are support rules of thumb. As new technology platforms evolve and people come to depend on critical technology elements, support will need to be adjusted accordingly. And, support services can be outsourced. For example, one company that offers such services, Netifice Communications, provides 24/7 remote help desk support for connectivity, desktop equipment, and applications, plus in-home repair and replacement services for failed desktop equipment.

Finally, who pays for plain old telephone service? Business long-distance calls are nearly always paid for by the organization. Many provide telecommuters with a credit card for use while telecommuting and traveling. It is becoming more common for telecommuting organizations to pay for an extra telephone line and service.

Be sure to keep accurate records of all expenses and purchases and read Chapter 4 for details on tax implications.

Some Final Ideas for Maximizing Your Technology Investment

Technology is indeed an investment. Depending on how much your employer contributes to the cause, you may be making the bulk of this investment yourself. There are, however, some things to consider when making your technology investment.

- **Buy products and services from sources that provide excellent customer service:** These days, the only thing that differentiates some product and service providers is their customer service. A live, capable tech support person has always been available by the third ring at my ISP every time I've called and has helped me solve my problems almost immediately. You will discover the value of this advice the first time you are paying 30 cents a minute while on hold for an hour listening to Led Zeppelin tunes.
- **Buy products and services with good warranties:** Increased competition tends to benefit buyers, often providing dividends in the form of excellent product warranties. The last computer I purchased offered a generous one-year service, parts, and labor warranty that I've already had to use. Should you buy an extended warranty on technology? The short answer is no. However, in some cases, a low-cost extended warranty may have value. If you do buy one, read the fine print to eliminate surprises.
- **Borrow some great ideas from leading-edge telecommuters:** There are a ton of ideas in the world of remote work, some of which can make all the difference in your remote world. A resource list is provided in the final pages of this book.
- **Don't trash your old computer:** A second computer is important to any driven knowledge worker but is an absolute must for a power telecommuter. As you upgrade your primary computer to the latest technology, plan to use your old one as a communications platform and backup. I use my 1995 clone for all my Web browsing, e-mail, faxing, and data backup. I use my Y2K hot rod with a large-screen monitor for word processing, Web page development, and graphics-heavy presentations. If one computer fails, I can keep working because I have the other one.
- **Get ready for more screen movement, high-fidelity sound, and higher bandwidth requirements:** There have been several false starts for mass access to a video telephone, primarily due to high cost and large bandwidth requirements. In the early sixties, Western Electric (now Lucent Technologies) introduced and test-marketed its PicturePhone, but it never took off. Thirty years later, AT&T introduced its VideoPhone 2500, which was also a market

failure. Videoconferencing has been common in many corporate offices for many years but remains fairly expensive and is not very portable. Today, with streaming video, high-speed connectivity, and video cameras on many new computers, computer-based video (collectively known as multimedia) has found a whole new start and can be expected to be fairly routine soon. The introductory ads for the Microsoft Windows Me Millennium Edition in Fall 2000 touted that "Home computing just got a little more exciting." The software allows you to store, manage, and share digital pictures, movie clips, and audio files. As multimedia becomes easier to use and more common, users will require larger bandwidth connections.

- **Expect technology obsolescence:** One problem with rapidly changing technology is rapid obsolescence. A perfect example is the personal computer. To maximize your technology investment, you'll need to buy products that are likely to be forward-compatible with their next-generation counterparts. Although this may be hard to predict, this is one more reason you need a good digital blacksmith on your team.

"Approximately 1 billion mobile Internet access devices will be in use around the world by 2003."

The Yankee Group, a leader in research and consulting services

So you're saying, "How can I predict the future of technology so that I'm not buying tomorrow's obsolete technology?" To help answer that, the next section provides you with the broad directions that technology will likely be taking in the next 10 years.

Ways to Prepare for Technology That's Not Invented Yet

The future is difficult to predict, especially with all the technological changes. Who could have predicted 10 years ago, for instance, that cell phones, which in 1991 cost about $400, would be given away? Who could have predicted that e-mail would be the most common form of business communication when most e-mail systems couldn't communicate with each other back then? Who could have predicted that the Internet would become so ubiquitous? Someone was probably predicting all these things, plus hundreds of other things that didn't come true. If you remain observant of major trends, listen to the more popular futurists, and make some educated guesses, your decisions will be more informed and likely more fruitful.

Technology is changing the old real estate adage touting location, location, location. Telecommunication infrastructure has for some time been a major factor in locating a new facility.

Giant private data-switching centers are being built adjacent to buried fiber-optic facilities to serve the demand for high-speed digital communication. In the upper floors of Macy's department store in downtown Atlanta, retail space was replaced with high-tech switching equipment.

This new use of real estate space represents one of many technology shifts that are occurring in the modern world. Here are other trends to keep in mind.

- **Voice and data transmission is shifting from wired to wireless:** Wireless communication is rapidly expanding, causing a radical shift in our connectivity to other people and the Internet. Home wireless networks from companies like, well, Home Wireless Networks in Norcross, Georgia, allow telephones, cable televisions, and Internet-connected computers to be used anywhere in the house without having to install wall jacks.
- **The computer interface is shifting from the keyboard to the pen pointer and to voice response:** The keyboard has been one of the biggest obstacles to miniaturizing the computer . . . until now. PDAs can display icons and text and can recognize handwriting fairly well. Today, some cell phones and computers recognize voice commands. Eliminating the keyboard is a trend that will make significant changes in the way we work, communicate, and play, allowing wearable computers, hands-free cell phone use while driving, and maybe even devices that rival the Dick Tracy wrist radio.

- **Software and instruction manuals are shifting from hard copy to download:** Many software suppliers are saving huge amounts of money by providing their software and technical manuals via download over the Internet. It is very expensive to duplicate, assemble, package, and ship software diskettes and CDs, especially if a bug is discovered and a revision needs to be distributed immediately. Online downloading assures that the supplier has a customer list and that the customer receives the latest copy of the software. This is an industry shift that may continue to the point that an original Microsoft Windows 95 CD and two-inch-thick manual may be featured as a rare collector's item on PBS's *Antiques Roadshow* in 20 years!
- **Software is shifting from one-time purchase to subscription:** Software is quite dynamic and is being positioned to be sold and used dynamically. It is only natural, then, that applications, products, and information be sold by subscription. Today, you can purchase a subscription for virus control, clip art and graphics, and automatic software upgrades. The next generation of Web appliances are expected to operate with subscriptions to such applications as news, access to games and other players, stock quote trades, and discount shopping.

"Today the World Wide Web offers about 21 billion pages and is growing by more than 7 million pages a day. A new study by Cyveillance, an Internet research company, sees the number doubling by early 2001. Likewise, the global community of users, now 275 million people, is projected to reach 1 billion by 2005."

Andrew J. Glass, "Internet's Explosive Growth Could Overburden Hardware," *Atlanta Journal-Constitution,* July 25, 2000

- **Transactions are shifting from cash to electronic:** As e-commerce becomes more common, as transactions become more secure, and as users become more comfortable, transactions will continue to shift from cash to electronic. Evidence can be seen today in the growth of sites like Amazon.com, eToys, Travelocity, and Egghead and in the fact that "the top revenue-generating online retailers are established brands such as Lands' End, Gap, Spiegel, J Crew, and Victoria's Secret" says the eCommerce: B2C Report from eMarketer.com. The report at press time predicted that U.S. online retail revenues for 2000 will have topped $37 billion.

- **Appliances are shifting from dumb to smart:** The microprocessor seems to be everywhere. Today, it's not unusual for an automobile to have over a dozen microprocessors to operate intricate systems. Set-back thermostats have been around for years to save energy, but imagine a system sensing when someone enters the room and making automatic adjustments. Imagine a dishwasher that notifies the repairman that the motor will need replacing soon or a vacuum cleaner that senses the flooring surface and automatically adjusts. These products exist, and you can expect many other appliances to get smarter.
- **Everyday activities are shifting from "off Net" to "on Net":** New devices, networks, and services will make it easy to stay Net-connected wherever you are. Expect to tune in radio stations all over the world on Web radio in your car or Internet access device. Video Net meetings will be common, perhaps even on your PDA. You'll hear your favorite music anytime, anywhere on portable Web music devices. You may challenge players on games at your skill level in real time anywhere in the world. You will listen to motivational talks, read excerpts from the latest business books, review chapters from the latest thriller novel, and perhaps contribute to a mystery novel as it is being written—all from your wireless notebook computer. Connectivity will redefine the potential of the power telecommuter.
- **Computers are shifting from smart to dumb:** Interestingly, computers are not only getting dumber, but the industry is now referring to a new breed of machines as "Internet appliances." What are Internet appliances? "Internet appliances are low-cost, purpose-built products that execute one or more applications that access the Internet reliably," said Jeff Thermond, vice president and general manager of the Home Networking Business Unit of Broadcom Corporation. The profile and purpose of Internet appliances will be as diverse as the companies said to be players in

the market, including Microsoft, IBM, National Semiconductor, Canon, Dell, S3/Diamond Multimedia, Virgin Entertainment, Sega, Sony, Nintendo, 3Com, Intel, and NetGear.

- **Team activities tracking is shifting from very difficult to routine:** A number of emerging products and services are now available to track work team activities and organize them in a highly usable form so that everyone can determine the status of each work task, event, and activity. When it becomes routine to track and record the detail of team and project activities, management can easily compare weekly performance data—from project milestones to individual work tasks—with baseline data to identify any trends and changes. The OfficePilot is one such product available from ExecutiveWorks (www.executiveworks.com). It is described by its makers as a Web-based activities management system that "provides an intelligent communications link and performance gauge between company managers and employees." This and other automated Web-based products and services are contributing to the revolutionary changes occurring in the workplace.

There is little doubt that technology is going though some major shifts and changes. What are the implications for telecommuting? I explore a few possibilities by peering into the future of communications.

The Future of Communications

In less than a generation, the business world has been transformed into a very different place, with new rules, and both positive and negative consequences. But many futurists and analysts see continued change, most of which will change your world as a power telecommuter even more.

Jeffrey Kagan, an Atlanta-based telecom industry analyst and commentator, was asked to paint a picture of what residential telephone service will be like in 10 years or so. Here's a brief summary of his predictions:

- Phone companies will offer wireless family plans so everyone in the family will have his or her own phone and draw off the family bucket of minutes.

- We will no longer be calling a place and asking for a person. We will be able to reach people wherever they happen to be.
- Broadband companies will offer local and long-distance phone service, cable television video-on-demand, Internet access and hosting services, wireless voice and data services, and more.

"'Virtual assistants'–sophisticated computer programs that can sift through information and solve problems–may replace the business executive's personal assistant by 2007."

William Halal, "The Top 10 Emerging Technologies," *The Futurist*, July–August 2000

- The future is all about access, connectivity, and interactivity. You won't have to dial-up your Internet connection because it'll always be on. We'll all be networked. Homes will be networked like offices are today.
- We'll be watching video news clips on our wireless PDAs, or any television show we want, by having our intelligent network agent search the Web.
- The local phone companies, the long-distance phone companies, and the cable companies will all start to look alike. They'll offer the same kind of services for the same kinds of prices.

What kind of tools and services will *you* be using in 10 years? How will you prepare yourself to make these transitions? Will telecommuting be so integrated into our lives that we won't even need to use the word?

If you remain observant, your technology decisions will be far more informed and fruitful as you advance in your telecommuting success. Irrespective of the direction a particular technology takes, as a power telecommuter you will be well positioned to thrive amidst change. With this in mind, let's jump to the next chapter to talk about how to make the most of your home office.

CHAPTER 4

Making the Most of Your Home Office

KEY CHAPTER POINTS

- Establishing your vision of the ideal home office.
- Creating a list of goals, projects, and acquisitions.
- Deciding on your home office priorities and needs.
- Planning your home office layout.
- Keeping your home office safe and secure.
- Understanding insurance needs and recovering from mishaps.
- Tax considerations for telecommuters.
- Preparing for the future home office.
- Using your home office checklist.

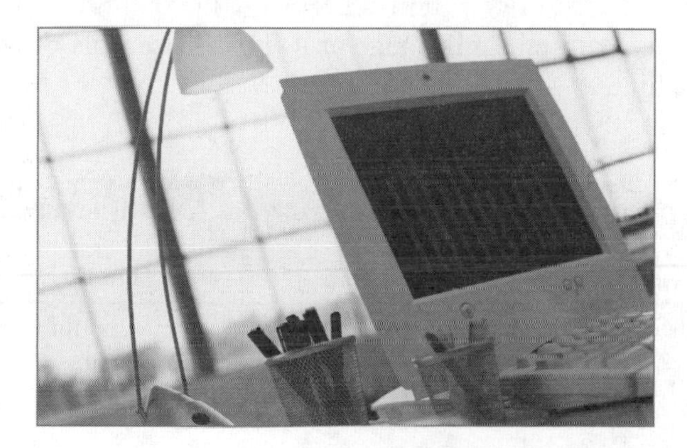

Establishing Your Vision of the Ideal Home Office

If your home is your castle, then what is your home office? To some the home office is a refuge. To others it's a workspace. To yet others, it is a dungeon. What is your home office to you? Do you look forward to going there or dread it? Is it safe and organized or a mess? Is it full of outdated electronics or is it state of the art? Is it loaded with filing you're putting off or projects you can't wait to do? You have a lot more control over what your home office can be than you think.

As a telecommuter, your home office should be a great place to get some serious work done—no matter how much time you spend there. To you, the ideal home office may be a well-equipped professional space or a quiet garden room isolated from the rest of the house. Whatever your vision of the ideal home office, *your* home office should remain a work in progress with you striving to make it ideal. To help you create the ideal home office, consider starting a "GPA" list: goals, projects, and acquisitions.

Making a Goals, Projects, and Acquisitions List

I like to keep my GPA list in a file (you can use a word processor or electronic spreadsheet) on my computer. Built from the home office checklist provided later in this chapter, this list helps me plan for equipment and supplies I need. Reviewing the list once a month keeps the items fresh in my mind so that if I see a sale, I can take advantage of it. Here's a sample of what a GPA list might look like:

Goals, Projects, and Acquisitions for the Third Quarter, 20XX

Goals	Target Date	Details	Done
Set up a project filing system	Oct. 15	Pick up folders and tabs from supply store	

Goals	Target Date	Details	Done
Begin recycling white paper	Right away	Research which recycling centers take white paper, what the restrictions are, if any	
Reorganize and inventory supplies in home office	Sept. 30	Use the checklist provided in the book	
Projects	**Target Date**	**Details**	**Done**
Add shelves for file storage	Sept. 1	Measure space and buy materials	
Finish office weatherproofing	Sept. 30	Buy caulk and insulation	
Finish building bookcase	Nov. 1	(See acquisitions)	
Acquisitions	**Target Date**	**Details**	**Done**
Image scanner	Before sales meeting	Must be the same or better resolution as scanners in the office	
Office supplies from headquarters	Next visit	Need pens, letterhead and envelopes, scissors, manila file folders, wastebasket	
Upgrade computer RAM to 128MB	When on sale	Determine the RAM type needed; watch sale papers	
High-capacity CD reader for backup	Next paycheck	Be sure it has full hard-drive backup and recovery software	
Bookcase materials	Oct. 1	Bring the plans and materials list	

You may have noticed that this list is absent of work-related goals and projects. As a power telecommuter, you will track those separately. (Chapter 3 provides worksheets to help you track work tasks.) When you keep your GPA list up to date, you will find it easier to set priorities, you will be more consistent at tracking and completing important home office activities, and you will get more things done on time.

If you are thinking "With all the work I'm committed to do, there's no way I'm going to have a neat and organized office," you are not alone. Many people in your position have let their home office organization priorities slip occasionally in favor of meeting a deadline. However, by your very nature as a power telecommuter, you're never satisfied with the way things are, and you're always attempting to do more. The challenge is to strike a balance between work priorities and office priorities because neither can be accomplished well at the neglect of the other. Whether you are a veteran telecommuter or you are just getting started, perhaps this is a good time to decide what you really need in your home office, and what you don't.

Establishing Priorities for Your Home Office Environment

Contemporary corporate office architects are faced with a paradox in today's work environment. The workplace must be stable enough to assure workers some consistency and meet their everyday functional requirements. Yet it needs to be flexible enough to meet the workgroup's ever-changing needs. Some of today's offices feature movable walls, informal open meeting areas, offices that are shared among coworkers, touch-down areas for visiting telecommuters to connect to the network, multimedia meeting rooms for intense project discussions, quiet rooms for private dialogue, and even a concierge to help keep it all organized.

Your home office should be designed with a similar level of flexibility. So, as you design or reinvent your home office workspace, consider thinking like an architect. As your own client, you'll first make a list of workspace needs based on the type of work that you will perform at home, the amount of time you will spend there, and the type of nonwork activity that may occur there when you end work for the day.

If you were an architect, how would you design your office for maximum efficiency and flexibility? Will you spend most of your time at the computer? How much phone time will be involved? Do you expect to do a lot of reading that requires concentration? Which reference materials and supplies will you need at your fingertips? Will you occasionally need a large space to spread out drawings or assemble handout materials?

In making the best home office, first inventory what you have and then identify your needs. Next, make a drawing of your office using the layout guide diagram in this chapter, showing the location of doors and windows, furniture, electronics and proximity to outlets, and other important office elements. The tips provided in this chapter are designed to help you in this process. With this drawing you will establish a visual of your plan, identify the elements that are missing, and implement your plan by adding the items you wish to acquire to your GPA list.

Running a Home Office Is the Ultimate Balancing Act

Good tightrope walkers are a sight to behold. The audience is always waiting for a mistake, but it rarely happens. As the performers advance in skill, they add multitasking challenges to the act such as bicycles, chairs, and partners to not only make it more impressive, but to increase the chances for an excellent payoff from the audience. The driven knowledge worker is similar to a good tightrope walker.

The driven knowledge worker is quite skilled at the basics and excels with certain talents, performs well under pressure, and is recognized for good performance. A power telecommuter is a driven knowledge worker with several additional daily balancing acts that are often unpredictable, increasing the level of difficulty. That's why you must be well prepared for telecommuting. The power telecommuter's challenge is to do the following:

- Balance employee freedom with personal discipline
- Balance workday flexibility with work output consistencies
- Balance quiet time with effective communication
- Balance efficiency in operations with effective record keeping
- Balance work activities with family activities

As a power telecommuter, you are responsible for attaining this balance. It's possible if you carefully plan or improve your remote office environment and pay attention to its design, setup, support, protection, storage, and contents.

And, don't forget quiet time. Having worked in a home office full-time for more than 10 years, I can tell you that quiet time is a primary source of increased productivity for the telecommuter. "As part of a personal productivity system I present to my clients, I teach the importance of taking a quiet time at the same time every day," said Greg Vetter, president of Atlanta-based Vetter Productivity. Vetter recommends setting aside 20 percent of your workday as quiet time, availing yourself of "uninterrupted time working on important and proactive tasks rather than urgent and reactive ones." Any power telecommuter knows that the home office environment is much more conducive to quiet time than an active main office environment, so take advantage of it! Chapter 5 discusses other specifics in helping you find and maintain balance.

As you continue your home office balancing act, I want to explore how to establish a system that identifies what you need in your home office and what you don't.

What Every Home Office Needs . . . and Doesn't Need

Just as every job situation is unique, so is every home office situation. In making the most of your home office, you need to consider a variety of needs, some of which may conflict, that require plans, priorities, and solutions to assure consistent, efficient telecommuting success. I have divided these needs into three interrelated types: physical needs, work efficiency needs, and creature comfort needs.

"The trend in the workplace is a homier look and feel. The trend in the home is to have a private, professional workplace."

Michael Dziak

Note: Some telecommuting policies have very strict guidelines on the type of equipment and services that can be used in the home office. Before making any big investments, be sure to review your employer's policy for guidance and restrictions.

Physical Needs

You need a good location: The ideal home office is away from the main flow of family traffic. A basement room, spare bedroom, or a little-used den or library can be perfect. Working at the kitchen table or on the living room sofa should not be considered a viable option. A window for light and fresh air would be nice but are not essential. You don't need a huge space, but it should be free of distractions. Your home office should be separated from your home in some distinct way. Some organizations require a separate room with a lockable door that will be used exclusively for work. If your home office must do double duty, your goal should be to isolate the room's other functions as best you can with cabinet doors, fold-top covers, or a decorative sheet. Several furniture manufacturers offer foldaway desks. It's up to you to decide how dedicated and separate your workspace should be based on how you use it.

You need consistent electrical power: The home office presents unique electrical power requirements that should be given priority consideration. The home office should be designed with proper electrical power, including adequate amperage and consistency to meet the needs of a wide variety of equipment. Equipment that draws high amperage, such as printers, copiers, and some fax machines, should probably not share the same electrical circuit as your computer. Local zoning laws, electrical codes, and a licensed electrician should be consulted when establishing or upgrading your home office. You probably won't need a back-up electric generator.

You need furniture adequate to the task: Basic, comfortable, and functional furniture is important, and the more time spent with it, the more essential are proper ergonomics. You'll need adequate lighting and storage space for work essentials. Unless your employer insists on providing it or if you need to write off some expenses, you won't need a massive marble-top executive desk and antique credenza.

You need supplies: You know what you need. Just make sure you have enough supplies and know where to find them. Be sure to keep spares of critical items such as printer toner cartridges, a ream of paper, diskettes, and postage stamps on hand. However, you won't need to duplicate the main office supply store in your home office.

Most employers insist that telecommuting supplies be acquired from the organization supply because it is less expensive. In some cases, however, particularly when the home office is a considerable distance from the main office, telecommuters purchase their supplies and are reimbursed. Check your company's policy to determine the preferred method before you make a big purchase. Unless you produce and mail a lot of physical output like proposals, you probably won't need a regular package pick-up and delivery service and a roomful of supplies.

You need your work items: Although you may be able to do some of your work online, most of your telecommuting probably isn't online. So each time you leave the main office, you should have the files, data, reference materials, contact information, and other critical work items for a given task. If you plan it right, you won't need to duplicate each project file, load a filing cabinet into your car, or drive to the office because you forgot something critical.

You need the proper technology: Your technology needs are also task dependent. You need a computer with compatible software and a means to carry or move data between workplaces. You need access to consistent electricity; perhaps an extra telephone line or two; a means of accessing e-mail and voice mail, the corporate network, and the Internet; perhaps a pager service and battery backup for your office equipment. You won't likely need a high-speed server, satellite downlinks, or a copy machine. See Chapter 3 for guidance on determining what you need.

Work Efficiency Needs

You need access to utilities: Extra telephone lines with nearby wall jacks and adequate electricity are critical to the home office. An extra business voice line assures your reachability, and an extra data line eliminates excessive busy signals, especially if you are online for long periods. Extension cords and shortcuts are not a good idea, even on a temporary basis. I encourage you to check local ordinances for installation requirements and restrictions and encourage the use of experienced professionals to install these important home office elements to assure reliability and safety. A cell phone can be an excellent back-up telephone if service is interrupted. What you don't need is a lot of extra gadgets and features that are rarely used.

You need an organized space: Your home office should be lean and mean, equipped with essential tools, work items, and information available when you need it. You need to separate personal items from company items just in case you get that new job; you can easily identify everything that must be returned. This also means you need to keep up with your filing. You don't need to be wasting time looking for necessary information or work items, especially if you are attempting to show how efficient you can be as a remote worker.

You need organized wiring: Wiring for home-based equipment can become an impossible and even dangerous mess without proper care and organization. In a well-designed home office, wires and cables are identified with tags, separated with wire holders, and properly bundled. As more equipment and communication devices are added, new wires should be laced with existing ones. In new office or renovation projects, I recommended that a conduit be added to accommodate future wiring changes. Unless you have very sophisticated technology requirements, you don't need to spend excessive time labeling wires and making diagrams.

You need a safe and secure environment: An injury or breach of security through poor planning are two quick ways to end your telecommuting privilege. Make sure your home office is free of hazards of all kinds: fire, tripping, falling items, repetitive stress, electrical shock, and even insects. Your home office should be secured against outside access, nosey neighbors, curious children, and neighborhood thieves. You won't need a security system suitable for Fort Knox. Later in this chapter, I discuss home office safety in detail.

You need power backup and protection: Knowing the importance of your work and its vulnerability to lightning, brownouts, and power failure, you know it is critical that computer and communication equipment have adequate battery backup (also known as uninterrupted power source or UPS) with lightning and power surge protection. Refer to Chapter 3 for related details.

You need efficient storage space: If you must keep large amounts of reference guides, sales materials, or product on hand, make sure you have an adequate, safe, and dry storage space. If you rarely use the material, hide it. If you need it a lot, keep it close. Equipment and product storage is frequently regulated by local home office ordinances, so be sure to check the rules and restrictions in your community. Unless the home office is your primary workspace, you shouldn't need but a small filing cabinet and bookcase.

Creature Comfort Needs

You need privacy: One major benefit of telecommuting is getting away from interruptions and distractions in the main office, allowing for long periods of uninterrupted thought and increased work output. Privacy is a result of proper office location and the rules you set in place for others (see Chapter 5 for a detailed discussion). If the kids get home from school and constantly walk past your office door or pop in to ask a nonessential question, your work will suffer. Privacy also involves security. If you are working with proprietary information, unauthorized access must be controlled. You won't have much need for screaming children, bored spouses, and nosey neighbors.

You need background noise suitable to your work style: Experts say that baroque classical music in 4/4 time low in the background stimulates superlearning capabilities. Background noise such as the radio, music, or the television is good only if you can remain effective with it—otherwise don't tempt yourself. There are those who must have silence. I personally need silence when I am writing or reading but enjoy listening to talk radio when I'm doing some no-brainer task such as filing or responding to simple e-mails. You don't need a television in your home office if you are easily distracted by it, and you don't need the ball game on in the background when you're talking on the phone to your boss, a coworker, or a customer.

You need the right office furniture: Comfort, utility, and convenience should be key objectives in selecting your home office furniture. Aim for the standard floor-to-working-surface height of 29 inches for your desk and 26 inches for the keyboard. Taking into account the type and amount of work that will be performed there, you should have adequate furniture for storing files, work materials, office supplies, equipment, files, books, and whatever else you need for your work.

You need an appropriate home office look and feel: When you thumb through a magazine that features home offices, you nearly always get a sense of the space at first glance. What do you see at first glance in your office? A well-designed remote office will be uncluttered and perhaps have a "control center" feel to it in which you can spin in your chair and easily access frequently used items or technology tools. You won't need to hire a decorator to match the drapes with the chair, unless, of course, you win the lottery.

You need effective lighting: Lighting is critical for providing a healthy workplace and creating the proper frame of mind during your long hours spent there. The ideal home office will have a window providing indirect natural illumination during daylight hours. Since many telecommuters tend to work beyond normal working hours, adequate artificial light is even more important. Lighting should be bright, soft, and positioned to minimize dark shadows. Adequate care must also be taken in lighting design to eliminate computer screen glare and other sources of unnecessary eyestrain. You don't need to go overboard with expensive designer lighting.

Special safety note: Halogen lights can be both attractive and efficient, but they can also compromise your safety. Since many of these bulbs burn much hotter than incandescent bulbs, a tipped-over lamp or too-close curtain could cause a fire. Always consider safety factors when selecting lighting.

You need proper air conditions: Fresh, circulating air and comfortable temperatures are vital to your comfort, efficiency, and performance. Take into consideration such things as drafty conditions; heat generated by electronics, air recirculation, and houseplants; and the benefits of ceiling or box fans. It's also smart to consider air vent location, the effect of zoned environment control, and the amount of time that will be spent in the space. Simple observation and planning will assure a solid foundation for proper home office air conditions. You likely won't have to reengineer your heating and air-conditioning systems to work at home.

What You Need Will Frequently Change; What You Don't Need Probably Won't

Recognizing that your needs are primarily dependent on your idiosyncrasies and on the type and frequency of the work you'll do in your home office, your home office will be as unique to you as your fingerprints. As you continuously improve your work environment, your constant challenge is establishing home office priorities. Use the home office checklist later in this chapter to guide you in updating and keeping your home office ideal.

The Home Office Layout Planning Guide

One of the best ways to begin setting up or improving your home office is to draw a picture of it. Below is a layout guide and content list to help you design and inventory the elements and features in your home office.

You may first wish to make several copies of the layout guide. Then, mark the dimensions of your office on the diagram and begin drawing the items you have. Using the content list as a reference, label the main elements of your home office with the number corresponding to the item. Also diagram the locations of doors (show swing direction), windows, and so on. If there is more than one of any item, add a letter designation (for example: first chair 2A, second chair 2B, and so on).

Home Office Layout Guide Diagram

Home Office Content List

1. Desk
2. Chair
3. File cabinet
4. Table
5. Bookcase
6. Shelving
7. Storage cabinet
8. Computer box
9. Computer monitor and keyboard
10. Fax machine
11. Telephone
12. Printer
13. Uninterruptible power supply
14. Surge protector
15. Document scanner
16. Electrical outlet
17. Telephone/fax jack
18. Network jack
19. Wastebasket
20. Recycling bin
21. Smoke/carbon monoxide detector
22. Fire extinguisher
23. Radio
24. ______________________________
25. ______________________________
26. ______________________________

Once you have completed your design, show it to someone else to suggest improvements and to be sure you haven't left something out.

Use the Layout Guide Diagram As a Tool

You can use this diagram as a design tool and a planning tool. If you are really serious about designing your office, make a few copies of your sketch, cut out the different elements you've drawn, and paste them in different areas on another copy of the layout guide. This way you can move your heavy furniture on paper and visualize reaching for files, turning around and answering the phone, and then spinning in your chair to work at the keyboard.

With the diagram, you will be sure to take electrical outlets, telephone jacks, and wiring into consideration when placing furniture and equipment. With the proper detail, you will also be able to plan your design to maximize natural lighting, avoid heater ducts, avoid conflicts with opening doors, and choose the best place for plants. The diagram can also help you plan for safety by including locations for a smoke detector and fire extinguisher.

Use the Layout Guide Diagram As Evidence

In most cases, I ask my clients to have telecommuters present their home office drawings to management in lieu of home inspections. Whenever you make significant changes, additions, or adjustments to your home office, show the changes on your drawing and keep it up to date. You never know when someone will want to see some evidence of your workspace at home.

If you are like everyone else, your home office wish list is much larger than your budget. Some telecommuters are fortunate to have employers who provide a substantial amount of assistance and support for home offices. As telecommuting time goes on, most organizations recognize the benefits of remote work and make an investment in its success. There may come a time when your management gives consideration to making a larger investment in telecommuting. The next section should be quite useful to you in case an opportunity arises for you to do some extra convincing.

10 Reasons Your Employer Should Invest in Your Home Office

I don't have to tell you that telecommuting can be expensive. Wouldn't it be nice for your employer to pick up more of the tab? Did you know that some companies pay as much as $2,500 to each employee to give up their space in the main office and work from home full-time? "Not mine, not in a million years!" you say? Well, don't give up yet.

Studies have shown that less than 50 percent of employers provide equipment and services to their telecommuters. If executive management sees telecommuting as a vehicle for reaching strategic goals, they will invest in it. Companies like AT&T, Hewlett-Packard, IBM, BellSouth, Nortel Networks, NCR, and Georgia Power have made large investments in their telecommuting programs, and all have reaped positive, measurable returns.

These investments did not occur overnight, however. As an organization gains more experience, as telecommuting becomes more common, and as bosses hear more stories about the positive results, management will tend to contribute to its success. If you need some additional arguments, here are 10 reasons your employer should invest in your home office. Some of these reasons appear in earlier chapters as good reasons for employers to allow telecommuting.

1. **To get more work out of employees:** Telecommuters tend to work more efficiently and longer hours than their office-based counterparts.
2. **To keep the good employees:** Telecommuting is becoming quite common among the most sought-after employers. If your employer wants to remain competitive and keep its driven knowledge workers, the company should invest in home offices.
3. **To hire the best graduates:** Nearly all recent college and university graduates have spent their entire student time as a mobile student, fully expecting the opportunity to become a mobile worker.
4. **To reduce expenses and valuable IT work hours:** It is less expensive to support common equipment than a user's choice. As the number of telecommuters increases, the cost of supporting them will increase as well but will be minimized with the use of standard equipment and software organizationwide.
5. **To reuse surplus furniture and equipment:** It is far more economical to provide surplus furniture and equipment to telecommuters than it is to store or liquidate it.

6. **To assure telecommuters have consistent service:** A telecommuter forced to make a personal home office investment will tend to take technology shortcuts and use low-quality, inconsistent service, potentially reducing efficiencies gained through remote work.
7. **To increase employee productivity:** The main office is a terrible place to work because of constant interruptions. The home office is an ideal place to work on projects requiring uninterrupted time.
8. **To reduce absenteeism:** There are lots of sick people in the main office. Working away from the office reduces the exposure of the best employees to illnesses that can cause downtime.
9. **To reduce real estate costs:** Many large employers have invested in employees' home offices, shifting a significant overhead burden from the company to the employee.
10. **To improve employee morale:** Making an investment in telecommuters sends a message to the best employees that they are trusted, appreciated, and worth the investment.

The point is, someday it is likely that your organization will decide to expand its investment in telecommuting, and when it does, you should be ready. You can do this by collecting new data and statistics that support the investment in telecommuters and by becoming a member of a telecommuting association or getting on the distribution list of telecommuting newsletters (see telecommuter resources listed in the back of the book).

Another way to obtain excellent testimonial information is to do a little networking with telecommuters at other companies, especially in organizations that compete for the same labor pool. This is one way to find out how other organizations have overcome similar obstacles. Also, keep a clipping file with articles as they appear, so that when the time is right to make your case, you are ready. With this information, you will then build a priority list of the things that telecommuters need and the benefits they provide.

Keeping Your Home Office Safe and Secure

No matter how much planning you do and how careful you are, injuries, thefts, accidents, and mishaps can happen. Do you have security in place for your home office and equipment? How well are you prepared for handling an injury or a fire? Do you have enough insurance? Are you adequately protecting yourself from harm? I next explore these issues and discuss some ideas on how you can be better prepared.

Chapter 3 lists tips for preventing technology gaps and disasters. This section expands on some of those tips and provides additional ideas on staying safe and secure in your home office.

Keeping a Secure Technology Environment

Feeling secure in your home office can be easily shattered with an unexpected intrusion of some sort. I'm not talking about your physical security here; I cover that in the next section. In this section I'm talking about protecting your work product, avoiding theft of or damage to intellectual property, and generally protecting your technology systems from mishaps that can require many hours of time to get back to normal.

Because the Internet is an information system with open accessibility, the potential for anonymous and unauthorized access to your data and information is still quite high. Because we regularly hear of security holes in the communications software routinely used today, it is prudent to take steps to prevent the loss of your most valuable assets: information and time. Perhaps this is a good time to assess your situation and consider some ways to stay secure in a telecommuting environment.

Technology-related security can be divided into four categories: electronic intrusion; familiar information breach; unauthorized access breach; and hostile information breach (or malicious invasion). The security procedures and precautions established by your employer should be your primary guide. However, consider the following as general guidelines:

- **Electronic intrusion** occurs when a computing or communication device is accessed by an unauthorized individual through a vulnerable "electronic window." There are many options for providing layers of access prevention, including passwords, callback modems, caller ID, encryption, and variable coding. Your information resources professional will provide you with prevention, detection, and reaction guidance for electronic intrusion. Consult with your digital blacksmith or employer's tech support staff for advice on these options. At the very least, be sure to require passwords to gain access to your computer, e-mail, and Internet account.

- **Familiar information breach** occurs when a family member either sees proprietary information on your screen while you are working or accesses proprietary information through your equipment in your absence. As a responsible power telecommuter, you can protect proprietary information by keeping your home office door locked, turning your password-protected computer off when you're not in the room, keeping proprietary documents hidden or locked in a secure cabinet, and emphasizing to family members and visitors the seriousness of any information or confidence breach.
- **Unauthorized access breach** occurs when computer or communication equipment is accessed with the intent to defraud or steal services or property. This includes such breaches as the use of long-distance telephone service, Internet access, or access to your employer's network by unauthorized family members. Consult information resources or network professionals for advice on access prevention, telephone service theft prevention, and other related access breaches. Once again, the best way to prevent unauthorized access breach is to have all access points password-protected.
- **Malicious invasion** occurs through the invasion of software-based viruses that can damage or destroy data. Researchers estimate that as many as 10 new viruses are created every day, so be sure to keep your virus detector software and operating systems up to date. Viruses have been known to erase or disable hard drives, take over operating systems, and activate just by opening an e-mail message. Some are self-replicating, some are activated by the clock or certain user actions, and as we've seen, some can rapidly spread throughout the Internet in a very short time. Consult with information resources or security professionals for advice on virus control or choose any of the several products from suppliers such as Symantec or McAffee that are commercially available.

Whatever you do to reduce a security risk, remember this: Staying secure in the home office is your responsibility as a telecommuter. This responsibility must be taken very seriously, and when dealing with technology problems outside your capabilities, don't hesitate to rely on professional support staff to assure that your technology environment remains secure.

Keeping a Secure Physical Environment

Thieves tend to be opportunists, and if it's not obvious that your home office contains anything of value—or that you even have a home office—it is much less likely you will be a target. You can do plenty of things to keep your physical environment secure from break-ins and burglary.

The goal is to reduce your home office profile and to use plain common sense to protect your home office valuables. When fine-tuning your security plan, remember that computers can be replaced but your original data cannot, so set your priorities accordingly.

- **Create a stealth home office:** Hanging a business sign on your window, putting out empty computer boxes, or working with your shades open at night are signals to thieves. I prefer to keep a stealth home office in which there is little or no evidence of anything going on or that anyone is home during the day. Keep thieves guessing whether someone is home by leaving your car in the garage, leaving the TV on in the living room, and using lamp timers at night. A low profile can reduce the likelihood that your home office will become a target.
- **Make your place a less-attractive target:** My dad used to say to keep the porch light on so the burglar can see what he's taking. Seriously, knowing that a burglar's best friend is darkness, keeping a 40-watt light shining near accessible windows and doors is a small price to pay for discouraging thieves. I like to use low-voltage lighting on a timer aimed toward dark exterior walls around the house. You may also wish to consider the use of spotlights that turn on by detecting motion. A colleague of mine even bought a device that barks like a dog when motion is detected near the door or windows. The less attractive the target, the more likely they're to pick on someone else.
- **Install and use quality locking devices:** How tough would it be for someone to break into your home? A lady in my subdivision was recently complaining of the flimsy locks provided by the builders

and how easy it is to get into her place with a credit card. When my wife and I moved in, one of the first things on our list was to install deadbolt locks. I took the extra step of reinforcing the thin doorjamb with some steel and longer screws. You can also attain additional security with a good quality, hotel-type safety hasp. Since the locks on most windows and sliding doors are fairly weak, I recommend the use of some kind of device that prevents the window or door from being opened. This can be as simple as a one-by-two piece of lumber cut to length.

- **Get a personal mailbox:** How easy would it be for a creditor, a disgruntled customer, or a thief to get directions to your home office? To find out, simply enter your address in any Internet map service (such as www.mapquest.com or www.mapblast.com), and you'll get a really nice map to your home. You want printed directions? You can get those, too! The best way to disassociate your home address from your home office is by contracting to use a personal mailbox or PMB through a retail provider such as Mail Boxes Etc. Use a PMB if you wish to have a local address on your business card instead of your employer's main address. In addition to having a professional-looking address, you are assured that someone will be available to sign for important packages if it is inconvenient to have them delivered to the main office. Be sure to contract with a service that allows 24-hour access to your box.
- **Install effective landscaping:** There are plenty of ways to use landscaping to stay secure in your home office. The first thing you should do is eliminate hiding places provided by large shrubbery or trees. Next, to discourage access to windows at ground level, plant shrubbery that includes a pain quotient. In the south, I like to plant fast-growing holly bushes near my windows. You can also plant barberry bushes, yucca plants, and other prickly things to, well, make your point!
- **Arrange for discreet package delivery:** A box displaying the picture of an expensive printer and sitting on your front porch can be a real temptation to a thief, especially if it's out there after nightfall. If you don't have a PMB, either install some sort of box on your front porch for deliveries or give instructions to the parcel professionals to

leave deliveries out of sight. If you plan to be out of town, stop delivery of your newspapers.

- **Make your valuables less attractive:** If somehow thieves do make it into your home office, they'll gravitate toward the items that can be easily fenced: computers, monitors, printers, portable radios, and so on. So hide the small stuff and make the rest unattractive. For instance, I've placed a "monitor defective" sticker on my good monitor (they can have the other one!). Although computer technicians cringe when they hear it, I've removed the metal case from one of my computers knowing it can't be resold that way. Burglars can be lazy, too. If it can't be resold, they probably won't take the time to carry it out of the house.
- **Install a security system:** This is an option you should consider based on your comfort zone and neighborhood. If burglaries have occurred nearby already, I would recommend the investment. A monitored electronic security system can pay for itself the first time it prevents a break-in. Be sure to research the various services since prices and terms vary widely. If you absolutely must sign a contract, don't sign for more than one year. Unless your employer offers a very generous expense reimbursement plan, this is something you will likely pay for yourself.
- **Make security steps a habit:** Property loss can occur through forgetfulness, an unsecured back door, or just by offering the temptation. Establish a routine for shutting down the office each day, using a mental checklist to assure that valuable materials, equipment, and information are secured.

Making your home office physically secure does not have to be expensive. However, not taking some simple actions to reduce your home office profile can be very costly.

Staying Healthy and Safe in Your Home Office

Any home office can contain a half dozen accidents waiting to happen. Irrespective of the precautions you take to prevent them, mishaps can still occur. Your goal should be to maintain your home office to avoid and prevent accidents, but to be well prepared in the event of an occurrence.

It is your responsibility as a telecommuter to maintain a healthy and safe work environment. Logically, telecommuters are expected to operate under the same safety guidelines established by their employer at the main office, so be sure to make yourself familiar with those rules. Safety in the home office can break down into prevention, detection, and reaction.

Prevention

Keeping your work area organized and uncluttered is one of the best home office safety steps you can take. This single tip can minimize tripping and slipping, fire, and many other hazards. The following prevention steps are fairly obvious but are worth discussing.

- **Never overload electrical outlets:** Home wiring and plugs can get hot and even burn if overloaded. If a fuse blows or a breaker trips even once, it's evidence that you need an electrician's advice.
- **Repair frayed wires:** Damaged wire insulation is dangerous to anyone who comes in contact with it, including you, children, and pets. Repair or replace frayed wires immediately.
- **Keep all wiring organized:** As you add more technology to your home office, you will add more wires. I recommend that you take a weekend day to sort and organize all wiring using plastic wraps to keep them in place.
- **Use space heaters safely:** If you need to use a space heater, make it a priority to do so safely. It is so easy to walk away and leave it on that perhaps you should devise a system that forces you to remember to turn it off, such as a note on the office door or a wind-up timer with a bell.
- **Install lightning protection for electrical, telephone, and cable TV wires:** Give serious consideration to whole-house lightning protection. Equipment-killing transients can come from inside or out, through electric utility wires, the phone line, a TV antenna, a cable TV wire, your air-conditioning unit, and even from static electricity. As discussed earlier, protection devices of this type have become quite affordable, and no home office should be run without them. Your local power company can advise you on products and services available.

- **Keep fluids and magnets away from equipment:** Fluids and magnets are the computer's mortal enemy. Get into the habit of keeping these things as far away as possible from your work area.
- **Repair or replace broken furniture:** If a desk, bookcase, or chair begins to wobble or squeak, it may be a sign of wear or damage. Check these conditions and make repairs right away to prevent unsafe conditions.
- **Stack boxes properly:** It's easy to forget about supplies or archived materials stacked in a corner. Boxes can only hold so much weight, and when stacked improperly, can collapse. Take the time to assure that this safety condition is under control in your home office.
- **Use appropriate equipment stands:** All too often people improvise equipment stands. All it takes is one bump from a chair to cause a top-heavy stand to crash to the floor. Make sure the stands you use are capable of supporting the equipment you place on it.
- **Properly handle and dispose of hazardous materials:** You may not think you have any hazardous materials in your home office, but you probably do. Many electrical devices today have large and small batteries. The materials inside your fluorescent bulbs and computer monitors are toxic. Common items found in the home office—such as printer toner, cleaning fluids, insecticides, and even plant food—can be quite harmful. These materials should be disposed of by recycling or according to instructions from your waste hauler.
- **Guard against work-related injury to yourself:** The power telecommuter takes responsibility for preventing physical injuries. Something as simple as taking breaks and stretching can help immensely. Keep walkways clear and file drawers closed. Consult with your human resource professional or office health and safety Web sites for advice on preventing eyestrain, electromagnetic interference, repetitive action injuries, and other occupational hazards.
- **Prevent personal injury to others:** You can minimize risk exposure by not having visitors. If you must, be selective of whom you invite. Keep meetings short, and under no circumstances mix booze with work, even after hours. Before a guest arrives, walk through the areas as if you were a visitor for the first time. Clear walkways and areas where you will be working.

- **Prevent property damage:** The key is to provide extra protection for items of significant value or that are irreplaceable. Pay particular attention to stacked boxes, items on the floor in basements, fire hazards, and other situations presenting vulnerabilities.

Other Resources for Home Office Health and Safety

For tips on ergonomics and improving health and productivity at work, see www.combo.com/ergo/index.html. The Center for Office Technology (COT) offers a booklet titled *Setting Up a Successful Home Office* (see www.cot.org/hoffice.html), which gives tips and recommendations for setting up a safe, comfortable, and productive workspace at home.

Detection

Since you cannot prevent things from going wrong, you must devise ways to get early warnings and have enough time to react to problems before they get out of control. Anomalies that could turn harmful in the home office can also be detected in a variety of ways. Give consideration to the following home office detection tips.

- **A working smoke detector is a home office must:** You've heard the stories of smoke inhalation fatalities that could have easily been prevented with a working smoke detector. This small, inexpensive device can provide you with precious minutes to keep a small problem from erupting into a huge disaster. Write the date on the battery when you install it and be sure to change it every year. It could save your life!
- **Install a carbon monoxide detector:** As homes become more energy efficient and tightly sealed, chances increase that carbon monoxide will steal critical oxygen from your living space without you knowing it. Something as simple as a loose water heater vent or an improperly installed space heater can leak carbon monoxide into your home. According to eHow.com, "Good mounting locations for a carbon monoxide detector include near a gas furnace, near sleeping areas, and in close proximity to the attached garage."
- **Use your senses:** There's nothing like using Mother Nature to give you early warning of a problem in the home office. Get into the

habit of monitoring for overheated equipment, smelling for abnormal conditions, and feeling excessive heat. Listen for malfunctioning devices and watch for evidence of damage or hazards from equipment, furniture, or nearly anything else in the office. If you detect anything that seems out of the ordinary, it's wise to have your digital blacksmith check it out.

Reaction

What would you do if you suffered an injury or had a fire? What steps will you take to protect equipment in a thunderstorm? What would you do if the power went out? Develop a home office safety checklist and make sure you have a fire extinguisher, flashlight, portable radio with extra batteries, emergency numbers list, and an evacuation plan for the home office. Some organizations use a home office safety checklist that identifies areas that need attention as an employee begins to work at home.

If you experience a mishap, immediately report the incident to your employer. You will receive instructions from your employer's safety program personnel for requirements, expectations, and remediation steps. After any injuries are tended to, your next priority should be to file claims and submit reports quickly and accurately. One way to assure this step is to keep some incident forms on file so that you can gather important detail while it's fresh on your mind. A home office inventory list and office photographs will make this process easier.

Being Prepared, Including Insurance Coverage

It is critical that you prepare for home office disasters, first by knowing that they can come in many forms, including fire, thefts, personal injury, broken water pipes, toppling trees, lightning, and locusts (just checking to see if you're paying attention). In addition to have a safety checklist, consider the following other ways you can be prepared.

- **Be able to react quickly:** If you had a pipe burst or a flash fire break out, what would you do first? In the order of importance, consider

1. Safety (develop an evacuation plan with at least two escape routes)
2. Communication (grabbing a mobile phone)
3. Damage control (only if safety is not compromised)

- **Have adequate insurance coverage:** Insurance policies are much like cars. Nearly everyone has one, but in the event of an accident or theft, each protects its occupants a little differently. Obtain a written copy of the policy describing what your employer covers. Then, make an inventory of personal property and visit with your insurance agent to assure that you are covered for any additional assets and liabilities.
- **Be inspection-ready:** A home office inspection or self-audit routine can be highly effective preparation for safety and security. Each morning on arrival at your home office, look around with fresh eyes and make note of how your manager would respond.

Home Office Inspections Not Required by Federal Rules

You may wonder if any federal government requirements affect your home office. You can rest easy that the Occupational Safety and Health Administration (OSHA) will not require your employer to inspect your home office.

In a national news release dated February 25, 2000, OSHA stated: "Home offices will not be inspected for violations of federal safety and health rules, the Occupational Safety and Health Administration confirmed today in a new compliance directive issued to formalize agency policy about home-based work. The directive, which provides guidance to OSHA compliance officers who enforce such rules, also states that employers are not expected to conduct home inspections either."

For the latest OSHA directives on this topic, see www.osha.gov and search for "home-based work."

Recovering from Emergencies

Here are a few additional tips that could save your work and your home office if something goes wrong.

- **Keep a paper backup of your important contact information and PDA:** Have you ever left your day calendar behind at a pay phone or hotel room? From personal experience, I can say that it's not a good feeling. Your itinerary, your contact names and phone numbers, the addresses of your appointments—all gone! I don't keep a personal palm-type organizer, but I often wonder what with all that vital information jammed into that little device, how could I get along without it if it were gone or stopped working? The great benefit of PDAs is that you can print out details vital to your trip. Before you leave, do it! I like to also keep a paper list of important numbers tucked in my briefcase or luggage. It has saved me more than once.
- **Keep a paper backup of your wallet contents:** Did you ever stop to think what you would do if you lost your wallet or purse while on a business trip? How would you get back home without a driver's license, credit cards, or cash? First, I keep cash and checks separate from my wallet. Also, once every six months or so I take all the plastic cards from my wallet, copy them, and put the copies in my day calendar. This gives me some evidence that "I am who I am." It also assures that I have a fairly updated inventory of my wallet's contents in case I have to cancel and replace credit cards.
- **Develop a disaster recovery plan:** Sure, you've probably had a mini-disaster at your place, such as a crashed hard drive, a power outage, or software that wouldn't work. Do you remember how much time you invested in getting things back to normal? Where would you start? Every home office should have a disaster recovery plan. You start first with an inventory, then identify a place to keep backups and lists, and then create a plan to execute a recovery. Here are more specifics.
    1. **Develop an inventory:** Set aside a Saturday once or twice a year to tally up and photograph all the key items in your home

office. Your inventory list should be made both for disaster recovery and insurance claims. You will need a hardware list (computers, printers, monitors, telephones, and so on) including serial numbers, a software list (including revision numbers and software downloaded from the Internet), furniture, expensive supplies, records, and anything else of value.

2. **Designate safe places:** Once you make your list, make a couple of copies. Keep a master copy in an off-site safe-deposit box along with master back-up media if you'd like. Keep your local list, along with back-up media; keys; telephone numbers of key clients, ISPs, and friends; boot disks; passwords; insurance policies; business books; and other vital items in a fireproof box away from your home office.
3. **Plan for recovery:** Plan for the worst-case scenario in which everything in your home office is gone. Your recovery plan should involve two phases. In the first phase, you will want to recover functions vital for basic operations: computer and software, access to e-mail, telephone communication, calendars, current projects, and so on. In the second phase, you will do what you can to restore systems back to normal.

- **Prevent disasters in the first place:** As discussed in this chapter, you can do plenty of things to stay safe and prevent home office disasters. Always remember that prevention is a critical component of your home office survival strategy.

Legitimate Tax Benefits and Limitations for the Employed Telecommuter

Tax laws the home office are like the weather: very complex, somewhat predictable, and constantly changing. One thing is sure, you'll need a professional tax advisor to provide you with accurate, current interpretation of both state and federal tax laws that apply to the home office. How complicated are they? I had a client who decided to allow some of their best employees to work from home full-time. For the telecommuters who lived outside the city limits, their tax status changed (actually went down) because the city charged

a head tax for any employee working from a location in the city. Since the employees were now officially working from their home offices outside the city, the tax was no longer applicable.

Home-based businesses and part-time home offices are constantly setting new tax precedents. According to the Internal Revenue Service, more than 1.7 million taxpayers claimed the home office deduction in tax year 1998. The Home Office Association of America (www.hoaa.com) reports that by expanding its definition of the "principal place of business," the IRS now qualifies a home office for the deduction if

1. It is used on an exclusive and regular basis to manage or administer a trade or business, and
2. The home office taxpayer has no other fixed location where he or she conducts a substantial portion of those activities.

At the risk that this information is obsolete by the time you get it, go to www.irs.gov/forms_pubs/pubs.html and download the latest version of *Publication 587—Business Use of Your Home.* Page 2 summarizes the home office exemption limitations. Better yet, consult your tax advisor or CPA for current laws and local regulations applicable to your situation.

A Tax Break for Telecommuters?

If you are a part-time telecommuter and hoping for a big tax break, you are setting yourself up for a big disappointment. If you work part-time at home and have some kind of office space furnished to you elsewhere, you will qualify for minimal-to-no tax benefits from telecommuting activity. In general, only full-time telecommuters enjoy income tax benefits.

Tax matters are nearly always the prime responsibility of the employee. The telecommuter must determine federal, state, and local tax implications resulting from remote work and is responsible for meeting personal tax obligations. As you assess your current tax situation, consider these tips:

- Consult the tax expert at your employer and a CPA before you make any decisions on deductions and exemptions.
- Keep meticulous records of expenses, equipment purchases, and business travel mileage.

- Make sure you are clearly delineated as a "full-time telecommuter" or a "part-time telecommuter" on your employee records to assure that proper tax status is assigned.
- If you work full-time from home in a different state than the organization's main office, generally, tax withholding and any employee taxes will be impacted.

Tax Incentives for Employers

Many states, including Oregon, Washington, Georgia, Arizona, and Virginia, have either proposed or passed legislation providing telecommuting tax benefits. One proposal offers employers income tax credits for the purchase and installation of new or used equipment in the home, including computers, fax machines, modems, phones, printers, software, copiers, and other work-related hardware.

Enlightened members of the U.S. Congress have made several attempts to pass legislation authorizing tax incentives for telecommuting employers, but none has been successful as of this writing. Although telecommuters benefit indirectly from the incentives offered under the plans seen so far, I believe that tax incentives will provide the final push to reluctant employers.

Considerations for Tomorrow's Home Office

As the commingling of work and home activities becomes more accepted, the home office will continue to evolve into a very different place. There's even a magazine called *House of Business,* which debuted in August 2000, that describes itself as "The magazine for the new home headquarters." If you are working from an established home office and ready to take "home work" to the next level, consider the following trends for the home office of the future.

- **Entertaining:** As the "home headquarters" concept expands, it will become more common for driven knowledge workers and entrepreneurs to entertain clients and friends in their homes.
- **Holding business meetings:** As more home-based "virtual corporations" evolve, executive homes with comfortable meeting space to accommodate a dozen people are emerging.

- **Making multimedia presentations:** Why not expand the home entertainment center for occasional business use? With the availability of high-speed networking, Internet TV, telephony, and videoconferencing, bringing clients home to see an IPO presentation seems quite natural.
- **Integrating work and family:** Very frequently, home-based work becomes a family affair. With available technology, unending e-commerce opportunities, and growth in popularity of such things as home schooling, the home is becoming the center of daily activity once again for many families. Feel free to make this transition as long as you can keep a healthy work/home separation as discussed in the next chapter.
- **Converting space for multiple purposes:** The home office of the future is one that is easily converted for multiple purposes. During business hours, it's a home office, and after dinner, it's an entertainment center or study area for the children.
- **Integrating information in the living space:** With technology, you can stay informed while walking from room to room. The *House of Business* magazine describes a Wall Street currency trader who has a primary "digital trading room" plus six additional screens (including one in the bathroom) that show international financial market activity 24 hours a day.
- **Providing day care/elder care:** As homes are designed to accommodate one and sometimes two full-time home-based workers, it is logical that additional space be made available to accommodate child care and elder care under the same roof. Professional caregivers would, of course, be hired to handle the required care duties during working hours.

Your Home Office Checklist

Finally, to make the most of your home office, I have provided a home office checklist for you to use as you set up and update your home office. This list also contains technology items discussed in Chapter 3.

Home Office Checklist

The Office

___Desk
___Chair
___File cabinet
___Bookcase
___Bookends
___Supply cabinet
___Tabletop space
___In-box
___Adequate lighting
___Fresh air
___Adequate heat/cooling
___Portable fan
___Ergonomic guide
___File storage boxes
___Wastebasket
___Pencil holder
___ ________________
___ ________________

Supplies

___Pens/Pencils
___Writing paper
___Printer paper
___Inked stamps
___Letterhead
___Envelopes
___Fax paper
___Mailing labels
___Postage stamps
___Printer toner
___Cellophane tape
___Paper clips

Supplies cont'd

___Ruler/Straightedge
___Scissors
___Stapler/Staples
___Scratch paper
___Disks and holder
___Rubber bands
___City directory
___Yellow pages
___Company directory
___Tissues
___Cleaning supplies
___Paper towels
___ ________________
___ ________________

Work Items

___Portable-work folder
___Product literature
___Reference materials
___Working files (paper)
___Working files (disk)
___Calculator
___Day calendar
___Telephone directory
___Calendar
___Work schedule
___To-do list
___Business cards
___Carrying case
___File folders
___Telecommuting policy
___Dictionary

Work Items cont'd

___Thesaurus
___Presentation slides
___Tape recorder
___ ________________
___ ________________
___ ________________

Miscellaneous

___Data security plan
___Safety checklist
___Smoke detector
___Fire extinguisher
___Flashlight
___Radio and batteries
___Zoning approval
___Evacuation plan
___Office mail plan
___ ________________
___ ________________

Technology/Hardware

___Business telephone
___Desktop computer
___Notebook computer
___Docking station
___Modem
___Fax machine/board
___Network card
___Phone/Fax/Modem switch
___Surge protector/UPS
___Printer
___Business telephone line

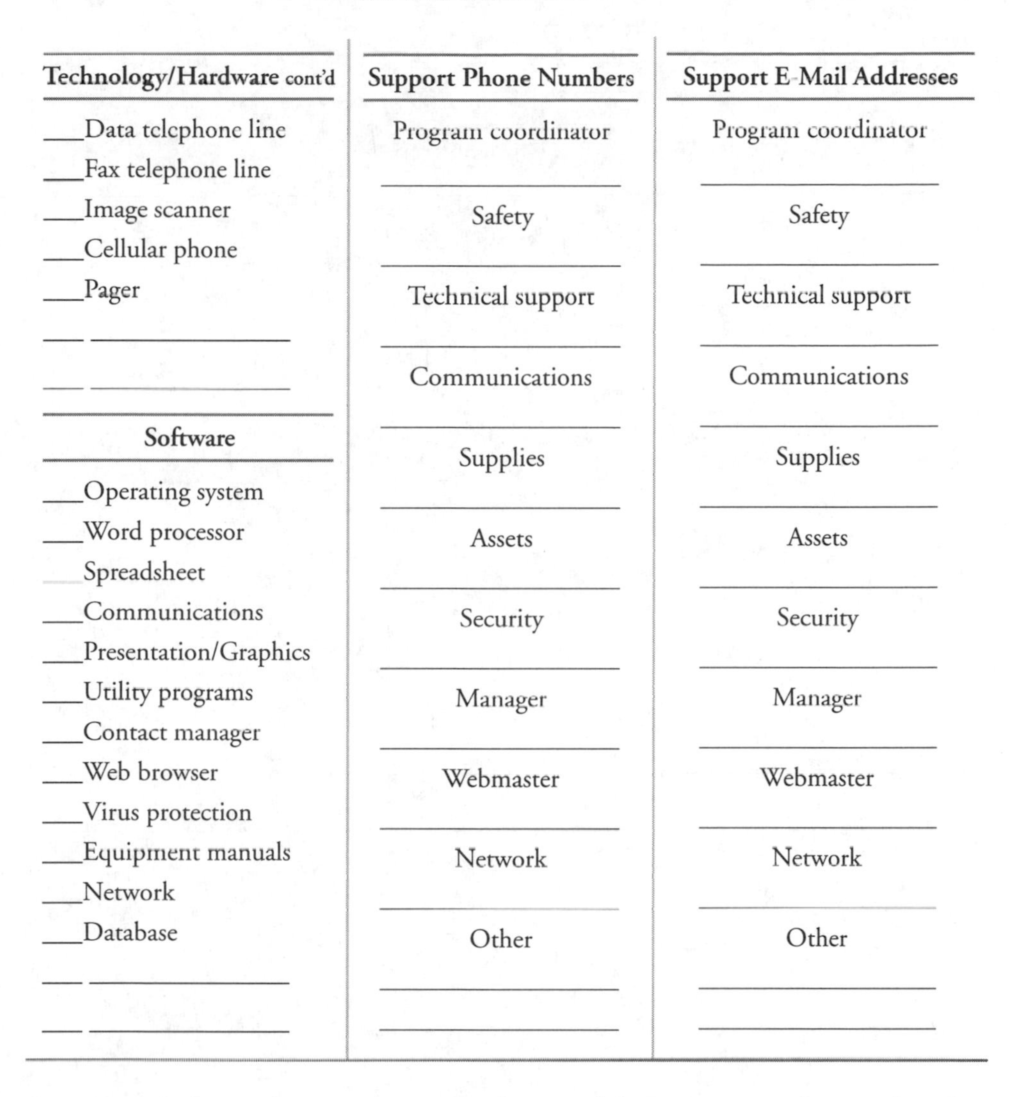

Technology/Hardware cont'd	Support Phone Numbers	Support E-Mail Addresses
___Data telephone line	Program coordinator	Program coordinator
___Fax telephone line	______	______
___Image scanner	Safety	Safety
___Cellular phone	______	______
___Pager	Technical support	Technical support
___ ______	______	______
___ ______	Communications	Communications
Software	______	______
___Operating system	Supplies	Supplies
___Word processor	______	______
___Spreadsheet	Assets	Assets
___Communications	______	______
___Presentation/Graphics	Security	Security
___Utility programs	______	______
___Contact manager	Manager	Manager
___Web browser	______	______
___Virus protection	Webmaster	Webmaster
___Equipment manuals	______	______
___Network	Network	Network
___Database	______	______
	Other	Other
___ ______	______	______
___ ______	______	______

As a power telecommuter, you are in charge of designing, creating, and maintaining the ideal home office environment. As you know, making the most of your home office is not easy, but the effort is well worth it. Start by establishing a concise list of goals, projects, and acquisitions. Face the challenges of your balancing act head on. Make decisions on what you need and what you don't based on reality. Establish reliable support mechanisms and research personal tax benefits and potential liabilities. Finally, take the steps, beginning today, to prepare yourself for your future home office.

CHAPTER 5

Creating the Ideal Telecommuting Environment

KEY CHAPTER POINTS

- Learning and practicing productivity habits.
- Training yourself and your coworkers, boss, spouse, pets, and neighbors.
- 10 time management tips you can use today.
- 10 ways to prevent stress and burnout.
- Relying on others to help you accomplish your remote work goals.
- Striking a delicate balance between work, family, and personal time.

Your Physical and Mental Environment

What makes an ideal environment for remote work? Do you need the absolute quiet of a home office or are you able to work effectively on a noisy airplane? What challenges or distractions keep you from optimizing your performance? What are some ways you could improve your telecommuting environment to make the best of this privilege? In this chapter, I look at some of these challenges and offer useful tips on creating the ideal home office environment.

Suppose you've established your home office, and you, your manager, your coworkers, and your family are past the novelty of your working away from the main office. Now it's time to establish a comfortable telecommuting routine and to develop a productive and disciplined environment in which your time is well managed. You also want a routine that won't burn you out and that will leave time and energy for nonwork activities.

No one is better equipped than the power telecommuter to balance and control the fast-paced, multitasking, high-expectation world of the telecommuter. Achieving long-term success as a power telecommuter requires that you establish your own standards, set rules for others who have access to you, and refresh your plans regularly. Clear goals, self-motivation, strong discipline, internal conviction, and dedication to success are all critical components of the process. This chapter will help you organize what you intuitively know into conscious steps, habits, and routines to absorb a telecommuting way of life into your subconscious being.

Practicing Telecommuting Productivity Habits

As a driven knowledge worker, you have excellent productivity habits. You've discovered what it takes to get the job done under the most trying circumstances. For you, the addition of the telecommuting privilege is like adding turboboost to an already fast car. It is important to realize, however, that just as telecommuting can amplify your best traits, it will also amplify the worst ones.

That's why it is critical that you identify and constantly improve your best and worst productivity habits as a telecommuter. If you take your bad habits home with you (procrastination, daydreaming, overbooking your calendar, eating junk food, and so on), they'll be harder to control. Consider the following ideas as you fine-tune your telecommuting productivity habits. Some of these points are described elsewhere in the book but are worth reiterating.

- **Work at home for the right reasons:** The most efficient way to telecommute is to work at home to complete a specific task, finish a project, or accomplish a certain objective. This way you, the boss, and everybody else knows your deliverables, and when you return with more work done than expected, you leave no doubt whether you were watching *Oprah* or the ballgame. That's not to say it's impossible to telecommute on specific days of the week or for reasons beyond your control (for example, ice storm, traffic backups, or ozone alert day); it just takes more planning on your part to do so. A reminder: Don't make a habit of telecommuting on Mondays and Fridays.
- **Be well prepared for your telecommuting day:** One of the most important elements for telecommuting success is proper planning and preparation for your workday. Get into the habit of updating your to-do list at the beginning and at the end of each workday, and make sure that you bring all the support materials you need home with you even (especially) if you don't plan to work at home the next day. Why not keep a "remote work satchel" containing tasks and assignments suitable for telecommuting in case you are forced to work at home unexpectedly?
- **Use the technology wisely:** Technology will never replace personal meetings, but when used well, it can enhance relationships and dramatically improve personal time management. Peter Keen, an international education consultant, saves hours—sometimes days—of unproductive time by using videoconferences from his home office to meet with prospects, clients, and associates. E-mail, voice mail, and fax are invaluable, noninvasive, timeless, and convenient communication tools when used well. Why not start attending meetings via conference call or drop your boss a quick e-note with

an update on an important project? Why not send a quick e-mail to colleagues to say thank you, happy birthday, or I hope your daughter is feeling better? These can go a long way to bridge the human-technology gap when you telecommute.

"By the end of 2008, we'll see 70 to 90 percent of households with high bandwidth Internet connections with video capacity."

Futurist Harry S. Dent

- **Manage your remote workload:** To maximize the telecommuting day, dedicate some time to workload and work output planning. Accumulate work tasks that are ideal for remote work and have them with you all the time. When you are assigned a project that requires quiet concentration, take it home and work on it there. For projects and work tasks that require frequent interaction or access to files, plan those for the main office.
- **Stick to your personal work rules:** Achieving a desired level of productivity while working at home requires that you establish personal work rules. When concentration is broken by outside distractions, productivity can suffer. These rules may include answering the phone during certain hours, checking e-mail only at specific times, no food in the work area, and no television or radio. Breaking your own rules can become habit forming, and even though you're not getting caught, it can compromise your basic work ethic. If you find yourself getting lazy or easily distracted while working at home, purposely spend more time in the main office to appreciate what it would be like to be without telecommuting.
- **Reward yourself for personal accomplishments:** At home your most positive reinforcement will have to come from within. The power telecommuter sets up a simple reward system that keeps the work process productive and consistent. These rewards may be a bicycle trip around the block, eating a favorite snack, a quick call to a friend, playing with your pet snake, or any other positive action. Rewards for small but frequent victories keep can keep you positive and motivated.

Although it's easy to take telecommuting casually, you must resist this temptation. For long-term success, the power telecommuter must maximize each telecommuting day by working at home for the right reasons, must prepare well for each telecommuting day, and must constantly manage the telecommuting environment and remote workload.

Training Yourself and Your Coworkers, Boss, Spouse, Kids, Pets, and Neighbors

Successful telecommuters have the ability to work independent of supervision and the tendency to perform well above the call of duty. But let's face it—telecommuters are people too! It is easy to be distracted by the television, the refrigerator, a sunny day, or an occasional lazy spell. Giving into distractions can also build up unhealthy guilt, potentially reducing your overall telecommuting effectiveness. There are plenty of ways to be highly productive in a remote work situation, manage your time well, and still take advantage of the flexibility that remote work offers.

Why Is This Training So Important?

A primary goal of telecommuting is to work in an uninterrupted environment, which allows for long periods of high concentration and thought flow. In an environment with constant interruptions and distractions (such as the main office, ironically enough), employees' flow of thought is constantly broken, and work ends up fragmented. When you're interrupted, you must take the time to reestablish your place and get back into the flow.

Long periods of high concentration and thought flow are very familiar to anyone who has done some work in the main office on a weekend or after most people have gone home for the day. Even with the best-equipped office, you must establish a quiet, nondistracting remote work environment by training yourself and those with whom you regularly interact.

Training Yourself

Working from home is not that easy. Without someone watching or checking up on you, temptations and distractions can weaken even the strongest person. Do you know what they are for you? How do you overcome them? Being honest about the things that are most likely to tempt and distract you is a critical first step.

If you know that snacking is going to be a problem, keep snacks out of the house. If a particular television show is important to you, set your VCR and tape it to be viewed later. If you tend to isolate yourself from others or are setting a pattern of overwork, get back to the office more often and set some workday limits. Whatever the weakness or temptation in the remote office, there is a way to cope, but only if you're genuinely interested in tackling it.

"There are many benefits of being able to work extended hours at home instead of staying until all hours in the office and making do with a vending machine sandwich for dinner while your spouse or family stares at your empty chair at the table. It's great to be able to do increasingly sophisticated, complex office work at home; it's not so great when we aren't able to close the door (literally or figuratively) on the home office and wind up working well into time we'd rather reserve for ourselves."

Gil Gordon, Gil Gordon Associates, *TURN IT OFF: How to Unplug from the Anytime-Anywhere Office Without Disconnecting Your Career,* Three Rivers Press, 2001

You wouldn't have gotten where you are today without a little discipline. But that's not all that can keep you from work. What about your coworkers constantly calling you with questions? What about the lame excuses for calls from your boss to mask weak attempts to catch you goofing off? What about family, pets, and neighbors who see you at home and presume it's OK to interact?

One of the best ways to overcome distractions is to stay focused on a set of tasks or work output goals. Telecommuting offers the flexibility to work on projects or tasks that require uninterrupted time. Discussing your specific work output goals for a telecommuting day with your manager is a way to help you stay focused. This way, you know what you have to complete, and your manager has certain expectations of your work product.

You will need much more than self-discipline to stay focused on your work. Your telecommuting training and experiences have no doubt helped. But, as odd as it may seem, to be successful in the telecommuting environment, you will have to provide some training for your boss, your coworkers, your spouse, your children, your pets, and your neighbors. Let's take a look at what's involved.

Training Your Coworkers

Gaining support from your coworkers requires setting some rules of engagement, staying professional, and showing gratitude when you come into the office.

- In situations where your telecommuting goal is quiet time and uninterrupted work, give your home phone number to only a couple of key people for emergency use.
- If someone needs to reach you in a nonemergency situation, have people leave a message on your voice mail or e-mail and commit to checking it at specific intervals so they know you'll contact them back within a certain time.
- Your coworkers should view your telecommuting activity as professional at all times. This assures that your time and privacy will be respected. In earlier chapters, I talk about never joking about doing nonwork-related tasks like watching the ballgame or doing laundry and telecommuting only on Mondays and Fridays. Coworkers should always be left with the impression that when you are working at home, you are cranking out the work.
- When you go into the office for meetings or for other work, be sure to visit with your coworkers, especially those who are extra helpful in supporting your telecommuting activity. Be sure to say thank you.
- Let your coworkers know your telecommuting schedule and how to reach you when you are working at home. This prevents leaving the impression that you are unreachable.

This coworker training is nothing more than common courtesy and teamwork, something that will pay dividends to you for a long time.

Training Your Boss

I know what you're thinking—your boss is untrainable, right? Not necessarily so. Training the boss involves a mutual understanding of your work expectations, good communication, volunteering work updates before they are expected, and regular reality checks. Keeping in mind that these techniques should be tempered based on the relationship you have with your manager, consider these tips:

- Until your telecommuting becomes routine, I recommend that you discuss with your manager in advance the work items you will be completing and come to an agreement on exactly what will be accomplished. E-mail updates can be highly effective in keeping the boss informed of your remote activities.
- If there is any situation during which your communication skills will be put to the test, it's with the boss. With some managers, you'll have to turn into a feedback machine, parroting all instructions and expectations until you both are satisfied that you are on the same page.
- Many manager-subordinate disagreements occur when managers come to their own conclusion about the quality of work without input from the worker. So, doesn't it make sense to provide work updates when you reach a major milestone or on your return to the main office? Volunteering this information ahead of schedule, especially if you've done more work than expected, will go a long way to assure your continued work from home.
- Be sure to set some realistic availability boundaries for when the boss can call you at home on evenings and weekends. "Unless you're willing to cut back to three hours of sleep each night and forego most of your vacation time," said Gil Gordon, "you need to make some difficult but essential decisions about how available you want to be to your employer and your clients, and how you can take responsibility for implementing those decisions." Anytime your manager crosses your boundaries, it's up to you to let him or her

know that, except in extreme situations, the boundaries must be respected.

- Make it a point to sit down face-to-face with your manager for a reality check once or twice a month depending on your relationship and geographical distance. Ask how you're doing, whether telecommuting is working out in the manager's opinion, and what you can do to improve. A regular discussion can keep the lines of communication open and prevent surprises.

Unfortunately, insecure bosses will have a tendency to check up on you at home. Whether it's a random call or measuring how long it takes for you to respond to an e-mail, some managers have a great knack for imagining you are going to get caught goofing off some day. In one instance, a telecommuter's manager made a surprise visit to the home office only to find the telecommuter working, but not at all presentable to the world. This incident caused great embarrassment and friction that may never heal. Training the boss up front could have prevented this from occurring.

Tips on Managing Your Meetings

Meetings are a necessary organizational evil, and for organizations steeped in meeting mania, they can become an organizational weakness. Remember when I mentioned earlier in the book that telecommuting can amplify organizational weaknesses? If your organization is bogged down in meetings, telecommuting can be highly resisted.

One way to mix meetings with telecommuting is to begin requesting attendance by speakerphone. If planned and facilitated properly, a meeting involving remote participants can encourage more concise communication, make time a higher priority, limit side conversations, and help the group stay on the topic.

Many managers dislike telecommuting because it makes it difficult to call impromptu meetings. Since excessive frequency of poorly planned meetings can drain organizational efficiency, it is important that telecommuting become a catalyst for meeting planning improvement. Of course, as an individual, you cannot change an organization's direction and culture overnight. But with the proper support from key managers, the benefits of

(continues)

(continued)

improving meetings by inviting remote participants can put the meeting improvement process in motion.

But don't think you are excused from ever attending another meeting. You should be willing to adjust your schedule for important meetings. Regular staff meetings where important information is exchanged and valuable peer interaction occurs can be critical to you as a member of the workgroup and should not be missed. See Chapter 6 for tips on effective teleconferencing, videoconferencing, and virtual meetings.

Training Your Family, Pets, and Neighbors

For family members, pets, and even neighbors, your working at home can be difficult to grasp. Family and neighbors may have difficulty understanding that when you are working at home, you are really working at home. How do you tell a 4-year-old that Daddy's not available for a question? How do you expect a dog or a cat to know the difference between work and not? Unless you establish clear ground rules and enforce them consistently, others are likely to take advantage of the situation. Remember, when you give in and suspend the rules, it's very difficult to go back to the discipline.

> *"Most telecommuters cannot isolate themselves totally within the household. They and their families can mutually agree, however, that the family exchanges routinely will take place during times set for breaks so that home workers are not continually distracted from their jobs."*
>
> Dr. Jack Nilles, *Making Telecommuting Happen,* Van Nostrand, 1994

The key to successfully training family, pets, and neighbors is to make rules right away and stick to them. When first telecommuting, take the time to discuss these rules and answer any questions, making it clear the critical role they play in your telecommuting success. In the case of a pet, establish very clear boundaries while working and reward good behavior. Make sure there are signals that distinguish work time from nonwork time. This could be as simple as a closed door, a work light on, or even a work hat you wear only during work times. Just remember: Contrary to what you might think, spouses, kids, pets, and neighbors cannot read your mind. It's up to you to communicate the rules and stick by them.

Examples of Rules You Could Set

Consider these ideas for the kind of rules you could impose to assure separation of the workplace:

Some Rules for Kids

- Noisy activities will be allowed after work hours.
- No interruptions unless blood or fire are involved.
- The office is off-limits without specific permission.
- Quiet while the work light is on or if the door is closed.

Some Rules for Neighbors and Friends

- Even though I'm home, during business hours I cannot be disturbed.
- I will not agree to let your repairman in or sign for your packages.
- Please don't tempt me to go shopping or play tennis.

10 Time Management Tips You Can Use Today

Highly successful people—be they inventors, presidents, military leaders, executives, actors, preachers, teachers, or homemakers—could not have been as successful without knowing how to manage their time. If you already manage your time well, telecommuting will help you manage it even better.

If you have some trouble managing your time, telecommuting will either force you to do it better or will make your telecommuting experience miserable. If you have taken the time to set realistic goals, and if you establish priorities based on their contribution to your goals, the investment you make in managing your time will pay off handsomely. Give consideration to these 10 tips on managing your time.

1. **Keep an active to-do list:** As mentioned earlier, update your to-do list at the beginning and at the end of each workday to assure that you bring all the support materials you need home with you.

2. **Always be prepared to telecommute:** As described earlier, carry a remote work satchel containing tasks and assignments you can work on when at home.
3. **Don't waste time in traffic:** When you go into the office or schedule appointments, drive during off-peak hours to prevent wasted time. Keep self-improvement, foreign language, or quiet music tapes in the car for those times you cannot avoid traffic.
4. **Use mass transit:** Another way to prevent wasting time in traffic is to take transit to meetings, events, the airport, and any other place accessible by bus, trolley, ferry, subway, or train. I get some of my most productive reading done when I am on transit, and you could too.
5. **Work efficiently:** Develop a work pattern that sequences work tasks needing focused attention to avoid doing too many things at once. Keep simple tasks at arm's length to work on when you're waiting for the computer to reboot or a report to print.
6. **Pay attention, do it right, and do it once:** When discussing plans or taking instructions, especially with your manager, listen carefully and repeat them back to assure that you understand each other.
7. **Stay organized and keep up with filing:** Establish a paper and electronic system to prevent wasting time and to find things when you need them. Keep your filing up-to-date.
8. **Improve efficiency through technology tools:** Look for ways that technology can increase your effectiveness rather than thwart it. Since uninterrupted time is the telecommuter's nirvana, don't buy a beeper if you don't have to and use a cell phone as an emergency backup only.
9. **Set up an automatic follow-up system:** If you do not have a contact manager program with a follow-up feature, develop a "follow up" accordion file numbered 1 through 31 placing "things to do" under the appropriate day of the month. Use this system for commitments made by others, for follow-up calls, for proposals and letters, and for general reminders.
10. **Be prudent and frugal with your time:** Allow enough time between obligations and be prepared to say no to activities outside your priority list.

Preventing Burnout, Stress, and Overwork

In the past few years have you found yourself working more and, while perhaps still enjoying it, constantly wanting to do more just because you can? It's the curse of the driven knowledge worker. It seems the more you can do, the more you want to do. Managers, in their ever-present drive to cut corners and get more out of their good people, have discovered they can cut back on payroll by assigning you tasks that were previously done by someone else:

- Have a word processor? *You* do the typing.
- Have a spreadsheet? *You* do the budget.
- Have graphics software? *You* redesign the newsletter.
- Have Web design software? *You* maintain the Web page.
- Have presentation software? *You* design your own presentation.
- Have access to the Internet? *You* do the market research, *you* make your own travel arrangements, *you* check out the competition, *you* find the best deals on office supplies.

These new tasks are added slowly and methodically, and one at a time, they're not that cumbersome. But eventually, you find yourself way behind on your projects. That's when the boss says "What have you been doing all day?"

Does this sound familiar? Without some kind of speed-governing device, the power telecommuter can easily become overcommitted—working 12-hour days, rarely allowing for downtime, and discovering symptoms of overwork. The symptoms of overwork manifest themselves in a variety of ways, including absenteeism, family problems, health problems, and general burnout.

Add a telecommuting option and it will ease the pressure, right? Sometimes. Empowering an employee to work at home can instead cause longer hours. This is not progress.

"Stress, which accounted for only 6 percent of absenteeism in 1995, jumped to 19 percent in 1999. What CCH, Inc., a Chicago publishing and research company dubbed 'entitlement mentality,' or a feeling by workers that they are entitled to a day off, rose from 9 percent in 1995 to 19 percent in 1999. Only 21 percent of the absent workers were sick, down from 45 percent in 1995."

Nancy Rivera Brooks, *Los Angeles Times,* October 3, 1999

Because technology gives the driven knowledge worker the ability to do so much more, it is you who must recognize when to cut off work to prevent burnout. Here are some suggestions.

10 Ways to Prevent Stress and Burnout

In these days of high stress, rapid response, constant change, and technology-induced information overload, humans are bound to approach overload and perhaps even reach burnout. Burnout occurs when you reach a point at which the amount of stress you are experiencing exceeds your capacity to handle it. "I can literally work 24 hours a day because it is always right here," admitted Barbara Lopez in an article appearing at myjobsearch.com. "I used to love my job," said Lopez, a technical support worker for a California HMO, "but now it never leaves me alone."

So, to prevent burnout, you must manage your stress. "Stress results from failure to adequately cope with stressors," said John Townsend, a professional consultant working in the stress management field. "Stressors could be loud noise, uncomfortable air-conditioning, debts, ringing telephones, broken relationships, unrealistic deadlines, discouragement, fear, pain, and thousands of other things that impact upon us in the normal course of life." See www.stresstips.com for Townsend's stress-reducing tips. Consider the following ideas for reducing stress and preventing burnout.

1. **Keep your skills current:** Continuous learning is a marvelous way to reduce the frustration of using the computer. Taking a software course when you upgrade to a new version can significantly reduce your stress and make you much more efficient immediately.

2. **Solve problems creatively:** Many problems often look unsolvable. I once had a problem in which my word processor would crash every time I pasted something into a document. I spent hours uninstalling and reinstalling the word-processing program only to find a virus in my operating system. By looking at problems from a different perspective, the solution can sometimes become obvious.
3. **Follow a proper diet and exercise regimen:** As a power telecommuter, you expect to work at maximum efficiency. If you are fueling your human engine with the wrong fuel and spending way too little time getting fresh air, your efficiency will surely drop. A proper diet is critical to keeping the brain cells active and maintaining energy levels. See onhealth.webmd.com for guidance on nutrition and exercise.
4. **Limit off-hour demands and calls to true emergencies:** If you can't get away from work, how can you possibly relax? Set some rules for coworkers that limit off-hour demands and calls to emergencies. You'll find that your stress (and that of everyone around you) will be reduced significantly by truly separating work and nonwork activities.
5. **Pet a pet:** Researchers have found that restless children, violent teens, stressed-out adults, and depressed seniors respond very positively to interaction with pets. Even if it's not your own dog or cat, if you take some time to enjoy unconditional attention from a pet, you may find your stress withering away.
6. **Volunteer your time for worthy causes:** There's a huge movement in volunteerism these days and there's a good reason. It's an excellent stress reducer! Through his volunteer efforts such as with the Carter Center and Habitat for Humanity, Jimmy Carter, in the opinion of some, has become much more fruitful as a former president than he was as president. You can find organizations begging for good volunteers through your community's newspaper or Web site.
7. **Participate in occasional nonwork or social activities:** I realize you have at least a dozen reasons not to socialize with other workers, but you might just discover that some of them are really human. Meeting occasionally with coworkers in a social event can bring down stress-inducing barriers and make interaction at work much more productive.

8. **Say "thank you" more often to acknowledge work well done:** Recognizing others for good work costs you nothing but can reap rewards for you and your relationships. The less you think of your own needs, the less internal stress you are bound to generate.
9. **Pick up a stress-management book or join a program:** How important is stress management to Americans? As of this writing, 5,167 books are listed at www.amazon.com under "stress." You can take your pick, but if stress is a problem, go get some information. You can manage stress with many approaches, from Yoga to hobbies, from personal trainers to traveling. Courses are available at your community college, on the Internet, and through your local park district.
10. **Don't shortcut your quiet time:** In the previous chapter, I discuss the benefits of regularly spending quiet time in your home office. Quiet time can also reduce stress. Once again, Greg Vetter, president of Atlanta-based Vetter Productivity, recommends setting aside 20 percent of your workday as quiet time.

Since stress is usually self-induced, you have much more control over it than you may believe. If you use these tips in your daily life, you are bound to enjoy more telecommuting success.

It Turns Out That Your Mom Was Right About Good Posture

Something as simple as proper Web-browsing posture can not only help reduce fatigue, but it can also reduce the chance of repetitive strain injuries (RSIs). Dr. Anthony D. Andre, principal of Interface Analysis and an adjunct professor of human factors/ergonomics at San Jose State University, recently completed a study designed to identify and classify the general types of postures assumed during Web-browsing tasks.

The goal was to compare these postures to those during conventional text-entry (typing) tasks, and to provide guidelines for proper Web-browsing posture. As a result of this study, Dr. Andre and study coauthor Jeff English offered the following Web posture guidelines:

- While waiting for pages to connect or load, change your body posture, relax your arms at the side of your body, or better yet, stand up and stretch. Don't hold the mouse or hover over the keyboard when you don't have to.
- Be careful not to plant the elbow of the nonmousing arm on the armrest or desktop. Instead, allow that arm to hang at the side of your body or relax in your lap.
- If you adopt a reclined posture while Web browsing, consider moving your mouse closer to your body.
- Take advantage of the flexibility afforded by Web browsing to vary your postures. Try not to remain in any one posture for too long.
- Time flies when you're having fun, so be careful not to spend too much time surfing the Web as a form of entertainment.
- You spend enough time at the computer performing work-related tasks. Remember that the "R" in RSI stands for repetitive.

Study details, including photos showing at-risk postures during Web browsing, may be found at www.interface-analysis.com.

Source: *English, J. & A.D. Andre, (1999). "Posture and Internet Navigation: An Observational Study." Proceedings of the Silicon Valley Ergonomics Conference & Exposition (ErgoCon '99), pp. 126–135, San Jose, California.*

Getting Ahead with a Little Help from Your Friends

Management trends, technology solutions, and business strategies are changing so fast that it takes an incredibly well-networked individual to keep up. Rather than attempting to become an expert in all the fields vertical and horizontal to your work, you already depend on subject-matter experts (SMEs) for support. But how good are your contacts on the inside? As a power telecommuter, you need close relationships with people who can help you out of a jam, provide you with guidance, keep you in the loop, and help improve your virtual presence. Consider the following examples.

- **Departmental moles:** Knowledge is power and sometimes a matter of survival. As your telecommuting increases, your chances of keeping up with internal activities decrease unless you remain connected with departmental moles who can keep you informed. Having advance knowledge of problems, changes, and issues or having a relationship with someone on the inside who can help solve a problem gives you a significant advantage.
- **Digital blacksmith:** I introduce this telecommuter's helper in Chapter 3. Much like the blacksmith who made tools for customers 100 years ago, find a computer expert who can make digital tools for you. A talented digital blacksmith can customize your applications, optimize your systems to meet work demands, design or find and install software that provides shortcuts to improve your efficiency, set up a firewall and back-up system to protect your data, and help you upgrade systems. It's well worth a monthly retainer to have a digital blacksmith on call and available nights, weekends, and holidays.
- **Industry guru:** When you are in the eye of the hurricane, it is often difficult to have an objective view of your world. It's really nice to have an industry guru available to call for ideas, trends, and contacts, and as a sounding board for problems and challenges. It's even better if this individual is outside your organization.
- **Reality checker:** A memo, idea, or proposal that looks perfectly fine to you could put a dent in your reputation. It is always useful for a second set of eyes to perform a "reality check" on correspondence that is plowing new ground, is repositioning you or your situation, is proposing significant changes, or will be seen by a large number of people.
- **Personal mentor:** Most power telecommuters have high professional aspirations. To reach new levels of competency, most self-help books I've read recommend finding someone who has reached that place and emulating that person. Better yet, why not ask for this person's help as a mentor?
- **Rumor control:** Each department in your organization, especially as the number of employees grows, has its unofficial spokesperson or what I like to call rumor control. Establishing a relationship with

these folks can help you confirm rumors, give you a heads up on impending problems, and provide insight on changing situations.

- **Logjam breaker:** When you were in the office every day, if you had a problem in the factory or in engineering or in purchasing, you could usually make a personal visit to get it solved. Since you are away from the office more often, the next best thing is access to a logjam breaker—someone you can call on an emergency basis to make that personal visit for you.
- **Executive confidant:** How often has a primo project come from the executive suites only to be handed to someone who is always in the office? One way to stay visible without having to be there is to have a relationship with an executive confidant you can trust to place your name in the hat and to keep you informed on important activities.
- **Mailroom manager:** If you don't already know it, the person who operates your organization's mailroom is probably the best-informed individual on just about anything. A good relationship with the mailroom manager assures that your mail will be reliably forwarded and that an important package has arrived or been shipped.

I know that as a power telecommuter, you lean heavily toward independence and tend to want to do things your way by yourself, but you simply cannot do it all alone. Give serious consideration to seeking the help of some friends, and I guarantee you will be far more productive and successful.

Balancing Work, Family, and Personal Time

A big challenge in the new workplace is the work-family-personal time balancing act. All too often one or two of these life elements thrive at the expense of another. As a power telecommuter, your challenge is to accomplish your professional ambitions and yet have a life. You can do this by deciding what is important to you, admitting that you can't do it all, setting some high-level priorities, and working to prevent priority overlap.

There's Good News and Bad News About Telecommuting

First the good news. "Telecommuting may be the first social transformation in centuries that pulls working fathers and mothers back into the home rather than pushing them out for longer and longer periods of time," exclaimed futurist Norman Nie in "Tracking our Techno Future," which appeared in the July 1999 issue of *American Demographics*. "As such, it has the possibility to strengthen the nuclear family."

Now the bad news. Being together under one roof more frequently is no guarantee of quality togetherness. Research shows a trend of more work and less family time. In the results of a 1999 nationwide survey of 4,113 people by Stanford University, 36 percent of respondents said they use the Web more than five hours a week. Of that group, 13 percent said they spend less time with family and friends because they're occupied online; 25 percent said they work more at home without any decline in work at the office.

Members of your family and close friends have some pretty strong competition in the Internet. It's fairly easy to compare the use of the Internet with just about any other addiction. It provides temporary escape from reality and can result in a focus away from other responsibilities. Some users find it irresistible, sometimes giving them a false sense of control and often being very difficult to quit. Without strong will and discipline or the influence of others, excessive Internet use can be a hard habit to break. With high-speed connections and Internet audio, video, and interactivity, the competition for time and attention is likely to grow even fiercer.

How Important Is Balancing Work and Family Life to Americans?

In a 1999 national survey, 97 percent of workers said the ability to balance work and family is more important than any other job factor, including job security, quality of working environment, and relationships with coworkers and supervisors. The survey, called "Work Trends: America's Attitudes About Work, Employers, and Government," is conducted quarterly by the

John J. Heldrich Center for Workforce Development at Rutgers University and the Center for Survey Research and Analysis at University of Connecticut.

"At the same time that work is becoming more homelike, the home is being invaded by work. According to the Families and Work Institute study, 16 percent bring work home more than once a week, up from 6 percent in 1977. . . . An AT&T study found that half of travelers either call in to work or check their e-mail while on holiday. Now the ever-present burden of work can be felt, quite literally, as the tug of the laptop on our shoulder or the vibration of the pager in our pocket."

Jerry Useem, "Welcome to the New Company Town," *Fortune,* January 10, 2000

Let's take a look at some ideas about balancing work and family life.

- **Make an effort to strike a balance:** Work and family life must be balanced. In a world where it is more and more difficult to separate work from nonwork, it is the telecommuter's responsibility to find the ideal balance.
- **Admit you can't do it all:** Striking a balance requires that you first admit that you can't do it all. Although as a power telecommuter this is against your nature, the consequences of not reducing your workload will lead you down the road to disaster.
- **Even techies must strike a balance:** Theresa Perry, president of the high-tech recruiting firm Atlantek Network, said, "The new workplace is more comfortable for high-tech folks. They have been knee-deep in the technology for years. Fortunately they also tend to be project-oriented and are accustomed to communicating electronically. One of the biggest problems is that they tend to overwork. Keeping a life-work balance has been one of the challenges."
- **Focus on what's important; set aside the rest:** Once you admit that you cannot do it all and begin setting reasonable and achievable goals, you'll have to start unloading some things not critical to your mission. The question is, What is your life all about? What are your priorities? Where should you be putting your energies? The answers to these questions are certainly not provided here. But when the

bucket of life is full and overflowing, it's time to find out what's important in the bucket and drain the rest.

And, since you can't easily make the bucket of life any bigger, perhaps this is a good time to establish priorities on what needs to be in the bucket and what can be drained out. After you set your priorities, the next challenge is to prevent the various priorities from overlapping excessively.

- **Turn it off:** Telecommuting author and consultant Gil Gordon says that telecommuters simply must remind themselves where the on/off switch is on the home computer. In his book *TURN IT OFF: How to Unplug from the Anytime-Anywhere Office Without Disconnecting Your Career* (Three Rivers Press, 2001), Gil offers the following tips for telecommuters on turning off work when it's time.
    - Create an artificial commute for yourself: As onerous as real commuting is for most people, it does have the advantage of acting as a buffer between work and life. A "commute" six steps down the hallway isn't the same. Consider taking 15–20 minutes to read the paper, go for a walk, listen to music, or do anything else that helps you disengage from the workday and reenter the rest of your life.
    - Make a "to-do tomorrow" list: We're all good at making daily to-do lists, but most people come to the end of the day with some items undone and others on their mind for the next day's work. Purge them from your mind by writing them all down and then leaving the list behind. When you do, it will be easier to leave your work thoughts behind also.
    - Turn your computer off: If you leave your computer on when you leave the desk at the end of the day, it's just that much easier to sneak back into your home office during the evening to do more work. Even if you only go back to shut down the PC, it's tempting to check e-mail one more time and so on. Make a mental contract with yourself: Once the computer is off for the day, it stays off.

So, now you are productive in your home office, you have trained those around you to help in your telecommuting success, and you have committed to manage your time well. You have a plan for balancing your work and your life, and you have started to choose your priorities wisely.

Now it's time for what could be the hardest part of telecommuting: effective communication. The topic of the next chapter is critical for telecommuting success, and I review some of the best ways of staying in the loop while working at home.

CHAPTER 6

There Is No Substitute for Good Communication

KEY CHAPTER POINTS

- Effective communication has never been more important.
- How are your basic communication skills?
- Practicing effective communication with modern technology tools.
- Etiquette tips for e-mail, voice mail, cell phones, teleconferences, and more.
- Tips on knowing when to use different communication tools.
- Improving communication is an ongoing process.

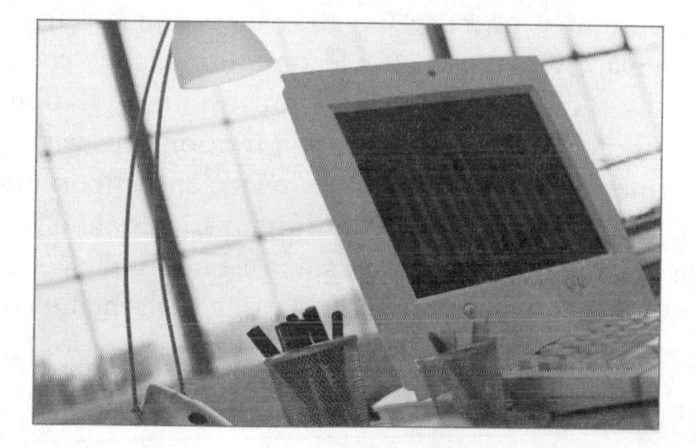

Communication Is All We Have Left

When you boil down the necessities in life, you've got air, water, food, human interaction, and communication. No matter how sophisticated technology becomes, it will always facilitate some kind of communication between you and someone (or a machine belonging to someone) else. Communication is both a facilitator and a necessity of the power telecommuter.

Effective communication has never been more important—and complicated—than it is now. With remote work, it is even more critical. Technology has given us some marvelous tools but little time to learn how to use them properly.

In just over a dozen years, we've been introduced to new ways of communicating through voice mail, e-mail, cell phones, pagers, teleconferencing, notebook computers, the Internet, palm devices, and soon to be more. So, who's in charge of training you on how to use these tools? How do you make sure you're saying what you mean in electronic correspondence? How are you supposed to keep up with the communication etiquette so that a simple message doesn't end up offensive? How do you determine the best way to communicate effectively?

As a remote worker, how do you handle your own unique communication needs? How do you know when there's an effective balance between "face time" and electronic communication, when to use different communication tools for different messages, and how to stay in the loop while working away from the main office? These are questions I address in this chapter.

The power telecommuter must develop and practice an effective communication strategy and plan. When you are telecommuting, good communication keeps you reachable. Governed by your personal communication etiquette, good communication allows you to maintain relationships with key people and to stay informed of changes, announcements, and important activities at the main office. A well-designed communication strategy and plan prevents you from "disappearing." Take a look at some elements of a good communication strategy and plan for remote work, starting with the fundamentals.

It May Be Time to Refresh and Refine Your Communication Fundamentals

Now is the time to refresh and refine your communication fundamentals. I'm talking about two fundamental skills: your basic communication skills and your skills at communicating with modern technology tools. Futurist authors Roger E. Herman and Joyce L. Gioia said that basic communication skills are critical to becoming a meaningful worker. These basic skills include careful listening, clear writing, close reading, plain speaking, and the ability to provide accurate situational descriptions.

If your basic skills are weak, technology will tend to amplify these weaknesses. That's why this is a perfect time to take an honest inventory of your basic communication skills and focus energies on improving them. Please don't blow this off as frivolous. Weak fundamental communication skills can act as a virtual anchor to weaken your credibility and slow your career growth.

In this fast-paced digital world, driven people expect you to keep up, and many have little tolerance for those who can't. Weaknesses are hard to hide for long. Rather than being discovered, go to work on them at a local community college or through a home-based training course. Some of my most memorable and useful college courses involved effective communication and technical writing. You will surely find it is time and money well spent. Once you have mastered your basic skills, it's time to apply them with technology.

Effective Communication with Modern Technology Tools

So you've been handed these incredible high-tech communication tools. You have a couple of e-mail addresses, voice mail on every phone, a cell phone in your briefcase, a vibrating pager on your belt, and a teleconference scheduled for this afternoon. You have a notebook computer that you use for e-mail, for impressive presentations, and for Internet access on the road, plus a palm device in your purse/pocket with a soon-to-be-added wireless feature. What more could you want? You're a fully wired, anyplace, anytime communicating machine.

The question is, how effectively are you using the technology? Back in the "good old days" when we communicated in person, in writing, and by phone, life seemed simpler. Those of us in the boomer generation were taught in school and by parents how to address our elders, how to properly write a letter, and how to answer the phone politely. Not only have many of these rules been relaxed, but new ways of communicating have been introduced so fast that no real rules have been written.

> *"Even with face-to-face communications, you have to say twice as much to get half as much understood. Without a plan for communication, distance can be prime ingredient in the recipe for disaster."*
>
> Eddie Caine, professional services manager for TManage

As a result, we receive e-mails written in all caps or no caps at all. We receive voice-mail messages that are way too long. We hear cell phones ringing at meetings and in church. We leave messages that are not returned. We receive copies of e-mails that don't concern us. We get a large e-mail attachment that takes forever to download only to find it's a photo of a coworker's dog.

Notice that I didn't say *you* do any of these things. As a power telecommuter, you are much too professional, way too disciplined, and too well trained to make any of these faux pas, right? On the outside chance that you are not perfect or have not been exposed to the finer points of modern communication tools etiquette, in the next sections I provide some tips and ideas designed to help.

Internet Etiquette (Netiquette)

As more people get online, it becomes more important that "Net" society establish and adhere to some form of behavior consistencies. The etiquette of the Net is called *netiquette.* How much information is available on this "obscure" topic? A search of the word on www.northernlight.com, my favorite search engine of the month, brought 109,683 page hits!

Netiquette can be viewed as behavior rules for cyberspace beyond the operating rules already in place. It's not unlike the unwritten rules of driving.

Driving etiquette may include exercising patience for an elderly driver, flashing your lights on a dark highway when you're passing a truck, yielding a parking space to a mom with a car full of kids, or a quick wave thanking another driver for allowing you to merge into a traffic jam. These actions are not required but are deeds that you ought to do.

Netiquette is the same idea. It consists of broad, loose rules that encourage courtesy, legality, truthfulness, respect, and other actions that the Internet society deems appropriate. These rules for communicating on the Internet (through e-mail, through Web pages, in chat rooms, and in interactive newsgroups) tend to make the process more effective, consistent, enjoyable, and even safe. Here's what I found to be the most common netiquette rules. Additional etiquette rules specific to e-mail, voice mail, cell phones, videoconferencing, and so on are offered after this section.

- **Do unto others:** When it comes to proper electronic communication, you can safely presume that at minimum, whatever annoys you most likely annoys others. So, the first golden rule of cyberspace is to govern your actions by what you would expect from others.
- **Respect other people's time:** In every communication decision, give consideration to how it will affect the recipient. Consider these suggestions: Decrease download time by reducing the digital size of Web page graphics and e-mail attachments; don't waste other people's time by sending nonwork communication; don't send unsolicited e-mail advertisements or solicitations.
- **Use fewer words and more graphics:** As an information medium, the Internet is more graphical like television than wordy like a book or magazine. Part of respecting others' time also involves keeping correspondence, Web pages, inquiries, and newsgroup comments word-brief and graphics-rich.
- **Don't be pushy in a pushy world:** In the rush-rush digital world of immediate response, it is easy to set unreasonable expectations of others. If you send an important note and don't hear a response in two or more days, there may be a legitimate reason. An individual may have had a family tragedy, been on vacation, may be ill, may have computer problems, may have 200 e-mails in front of yours, or may not have received your request in the first place. If you must

have an answer, consider opening a second request with "In case you had not received my correspondence for some reason."

- **Keep your virus software up to date and scan regularly:** Popular virus-scanning software is updated as soon as a new virus is detected. Updating your software and scanning for viruses regularly provides protection from some real problems. Since many recent viruses featured self-replicating software that caused the destructive virus to be sent to everyone in the victim's e-mail address book, you'll be protecting others as well.
- **Acknowledge the source of materials not your own:** Information and protected material are so accessible on the Internet that "using and sharing" can easily develop into "stealing and illegal distribution" if you are not careful. To be safe, ask for permission and acknowledge the source of information and protected material that you use or forward.
- **Use what you own, pay for what you use:** Technology makes it incredibly easy to create an illegal copy of software or not pay for shareware. Although it's tempting (and illegal) to take shortcuts, a key netiquette rule is to use only legitimate copies of software in your work and personal activities. Also, never abuse your employer's Internet access service, high-speed connection, software, news and research services, and so on through excessive personal use.
- **Don't put your professional persona at risk:** Once the written word is committed to cyberspace, there is no telling where it might turn up again. You can set your own digital persona standards by steering clear of foul language, harsh criticism, blatant self-promotion, writing without thinking, and telling half-truths (which are really half-lies). Also remember that cyber-revenge is fairly uncomplicated but can be costly if you make the wrong person mad.
- **Don't release personal information to strangers:** This may seem obvious, but once personal information is in cyberspace—especially if it's incorrect or damaging or makes you vulnerable—it can be painfully difficult to remove. Releasing information such as a telephone number or street address to those who you believe to be legitimate should be done at your own risk. Keep your personal information to yourself as much as possible.

- **Consider the human:** Behind every screen name or e-mail address is a real person who could be anywhere in the world. If you must disagree with someone online, do it with dignity and respect. There is all too much evidence of writers "flaming" others in correspondence, a practice in which people unreasonably criticize and berate others for differing opinions. Because the Internet is an international medium, remember that some common phrases and local slang do not translate well to other languages. If you remain aware in all your communication that a person is on the receiving end, you will more likely make the right netiquette decision.

As a power telecommuter, it is critical that you follow the basic rules of netiquette for maintaining a professional image, retaining respect, and staying in the loop. If you would like more details on these and other rules, enter "netiquette" into any search engine for surprisingly plentiful resources.

E-Mail Etiquette

It's fairly easy for regular users of e-mail, including myself, to take for granted the ability to communicate with others around the world with the click of a mouse. It wasn't all that long ago, however, that a client of mine had three corporate divisions with three separate e-mail systems that could not communicate with each other or the rest of the business world.

Internet-based universal e-mail, which has been around for a relatively short time, changed all that. As recently as January 1993, *CommunicationsWeek* magazine exclaimed in apparent wonderment, "With consistent interfaces and a unified e-mail backbone, users could exchange virtually any type of data in virtually any format using a common, easy-to-use interface." Today, to be without an e-mail address on a business card is a rare occurrence.

The Problem with E-Mail

Because telecommuters rely on e-mail as a primary communication medium, it is especially critical to use it correctly and effectively. The problem with e-mail is that it depends on text to communicate the message. Although this is not that big a deal for most business communication, it is important to understand its limitations and when to best use it for communicating. While e-mail is ideal for all kinds of business and personal communication, sensitive issues should be handled face-to-face. I offer some guidance on when to use various communication media for different situations at the end of this chapter.

Another e-mail limitation is that it is fairly easy to distract a reader from your message or offend someone by breaking simple etiquette rules. As a power telecommuter, you will find that it's best to keep all correspondence professional and follow e-mail etiquette do's and don'ts.

Be Careful with Emoticons

Adding typed expressions (called *emoticons*) such as smiles :-) or winks ;-) can be cute but is effective in professional communication under limited circumstances.

If you must see more emoticons, take a look at wellweb.com/behappy/smiley.htm for all the smiley options you could ever need.

E-Mail Do's and Don'ts

As I'm sure you know, you can unintentionally annoy or offend other people by simply sending an e-mail message. Part of being a power telecommuter is remaining aware of proper e-mail etiquette and practicing its rules. Here are some e-mail do's and don'ts you should consider as you refresh and refine your e-mail communication fundamentals.

E-Mail Do's:

- Limit communication on your business e-mail service to business correspondence.
- When sending an e-mail, include a succinct subject or topic reference title.
- Be polite, concise, professional, businesslike, and direct in all your correspondence.

- Compress large attachments or avoid them altogether.
- If you expect an answer to your correspondence, establish clear (what do you want to know?) and precise (when do you want it?) response expectations.
- If you are away for more than a day or two, set up an automatic response indicating when you will return messages.
- Use urgent and priority flags sparingly and only when such emphasis is warranted.
- Include a salutation block with your "signature," title, mailing address, and phone number. Some e-mail applications can do this for you automatically.
- Before sending a message, review it carefully for proper grammar, accurate spelling (set your software for automatic spell-check), clarity, and tone.
- Read all e-mail messages carefully. In my haste to reply under time pressures, I find it is easy to skip over key communications or important instructions.
- Respond to all e-mails promptly, at least within 24-hours.
- If responding to a message, include the writer's message in your reply to assure the context is retained.
- Request to be removed from unwanted distribution lists immedi ately, especially those on nonwork-related topics.
- Never open an attachment from an unknown sender. A computer virus or worm can be executed in this way.
- Report suspicious, unusual, or unlawful e-mail activity to your information services professionals.

E-Mail Don'ts:

- Don't type in all caps because it IMPLIES SHOUTING.
- Don't send messages without proper capitalization or punctuation. It conveys unprofessionalism.
- Don't send important messages without taking a minimum 10-minute certainty break. After you write your note and set up the

send, do something else for 10 minutes and then reread it thoroughly. This assures that you're sending exactly what you want to send.

- Don't forget the attachment. From frequent personal experience, I know it can be embarrassing to send a second e-mail message with the note "And now, here's the attachment I promised."
- Don't reply to "all recipients" unless it is appropriate that everyone see your reply.
- Don't compromise your recipients' privacy. If you are sending a message to a list of people, enter your own name in the "send to" section, then enter all other recipient names in the "bcc" (blind carbon copy) section. Using bcc, their names and addresses won't appear on anyone else's copy.
- Don't use sarcasm. Without voice intonations, facial expressions, or the wink of an eye, sarcasm can be indistinguishable from normal dialogue.
- Don't send personal messages to work-related recipient lists.
- Don't send or forward jokes, chain letters, or get-rich schemes.

As you can see, these e-mail do's and don'ts are common sense. When using e-mail, the bottom line is use it wisely, send what you intend, keep it professional, respect your recipients, and remain aware of the risks.

One more thing you should remember: E-mail correspondence is not private. Especially when you work for an employer, use your e-mail as if someone is constantly monitoring your messages. Interestingly, many of the same commonsense netiquette rules apply to voice mail, which I cover next.

Instant Messaging: Telecommuter's Tool or Telecommuter's Trouble?

One telecommuting benefit is working in an uninterrupted environment. This allows long periods of concentrated thought, which often results in significant productivity increases. *Instant messaging* is a network-based tool that could change all that if not used judiciously. Instant messaging allows anyone with a node on a properly equipped network the ability to send a message to someone else on the network and begin a live keyboard conversation.

Some say that instant messaging can fill telecommuters' need for random "water cooler" interactions with colleagues. The system lets users "see" who is signed on the network, allowing instant communication through the keyboard. Although I see the benefits of random interaction among colleagues on business matters, this nonwork activity can become distracting and possibly abused.

Just as I recommend that you turn off an audible notice of e-mail so that you don't become a reactionary slave, I offer the same advice for instant messaging. If your goal is to enjoy uninterrupted time in your home office, take control by turning off the instant-messaging feature. Lest your colleagues conclude that you are ignoring them when you don't respond to their instant messages, let those who use instant messaging know that you will respond to these inquiries when you regularly check e-mail.

Voice-Mail Etiquette

Even though voice mail has been in mass use since the early eighties, I think you will agree that too many people are still making up their own rules for it, and too many annoying habits are being practiced. If you are thinking "I've been using voice mail for years; what could I possibly learn?" humor me on this. There may be something here that could give you an edge as a power telecommuter. Although I don't pretend to have all the answers, please consider the following commonsense voice-mail rules.

- **Record useful information in your greeting:** Since your voice-mail greeting is frequently the first impression you leave, make it count. Thank the caller, announce your name and company name, and request a brief but detailed message. It is preferable (but sometimes difficult to keep up) to record a greeting each morning stating today's date, whether you're available, when to expect a return call, and other useful details. If you are telecommuting, I prefer that you say "I'm working away from the office today" as opposed to "I'm at home today," since telecommuting skeptics could jump to the wrong conclusion. Advise those who call you frequently to press the # key to bypass your greeting if your system has that feature. In some cases, it is useful to say who to call for urgent matters. Of course you should avoid lengthy greetings, keeping them between 10 and 15 seconds long.

- **Leave useful information in your message:** It is much more efficient to leave information of substance in your message so that the called person knows how to respond. The "call me" or "I'm returning your call" method of voice mail is not very efficient. When leaving a message, say your name (and your company name if the person doesn't know you), your call's purpose or the information you need, plus the best way to reach you *and* the best time to call you back. Except for a few close acquaintances, I always leave my telephone number in case the person is unable to access his or her personal phone directory. Many voice-mail systems offer delivery and playback options, so I always press 1 after I leave a message in case I wish to take advantage of them.
- **Don't send callers to voice-mail jail:** We've all experienced this: "If you have a technical problem press 1. If you have a billing problem press 2." Then, when you get to the next layer, and the next layer, you get a whole new set of choices. Do what you can to avoid these situations. A "follow me" telephone system, which tries different phones until it finds you, can be just as frustrating to a caller—especially when there is silence during the transfer process. If you have one of these systems, call yourself and listen to what your callers hear and make it better. It's common for a recording to come up two or three times and say, "I'm sorry, I can't come to the phone right now," because the user programmed it incorrectly.

> *"The problem with getting in touch with some mobile workers is that they have a variety of phone numbers depending on their schedule for the day. To make yourself easier to reach, give one central phone number to your clients or business associates and forward calls from that number to wherever you will be that day. The person who is trying to reach you shouldn't have to know your schedule or hunt you down."*
>
> Phil Montero, founder of YouCanWorkFromAnywhere.com

- **Say your phone number so that it can be written down:** This is one of my pet peeves. When leaving a message, say your telephone number slowly, pausing where there are natural breaks. If callers have one chance to write down the information, they are likely to miss your phone number if you rattle off all 10 digits at once. I've been tempted to call back people who leave such messages and say my phone number so quickly that it would be impossible to write down. (I have so far resisted the temptation.)
- **Please don't end your greeting with "Have a nice day!":** Each time I hear this, I picture a big yellow smiley face. Unless it is a clever part of your corporate positioning campaign, adding a phrase at the end of your greeting wastes valuable phone time and can sound phony.
- **Keep your messages brief:** It's a rare situation in which you will need to leave a lengthy message. We've all had people ramble on until the voice mail times out, and sure enough, they call back and ramble some more. If people are out of town and checking voice mail from an airport or gas station pay phone, the last thing they have time for is a five-minute message, especially if they have to hear it over and over to listen to other messages. If you can't say it in 30 to 45 seconds, send an e-mail.
- **Avoid screening your calls:** I know that while you are telecommuting it is tempting to screen calls by listening to messages as they come in and then answering only the ones you want. I also know that one of your primary goals in the home office is uninterrupted work. However, some people take such offense to call screening that getting caught at it could change their trust in you. If you must not be disturbed while you are working on an important project,

program your phone to send calls directly to voice mail and answer them later.

- **Use a system that forwards calls to voice mail while you are on the phone:** Call waiting is a nice feature, but constant interruptions to a critical discussion can become annoying and distracting. I believe that when you are talking with someone by phone, a certain privacy and personal connection are established. This is especially true in our mobile world where it is so difficult to reach someone by phone. When a call-waiting signal causes you to abruptly interrupt the conversation, it can leave the impression that the other person is no longer significant. An excellent solution is to use a system that forwards calls to voice mail while you are on the phone. Such systems are available from nearly all local telephone companies.
- **Disable call waiting before making important calls:** Did you know that you can disable call waiting? In many telephone systems, you simply dial *70 (check with your local telephone company) before you dial the number, and anyone who attempts to reach you while you are on that call will get a busy signal or will be sent to voice mail. Many people program their computer to dial *70 before their Internet service provider dial-in number to prevent call waiting from disconnecting them while online.

As new communication technology emerges, your ability to remain mobile and in touch will increase. The key is to adopt and use new technology in a way that allows you to be reachable without jeopardizing your relationships and to continue leading a quality personal life. Speaking of mobility, cell phones have brought not only new freedom but also a new set of annoyances and etiquette. I review them next.

Cell-Phone Etiquette

You've seen them: the cell-phone zombies. They walk around in the mall, bump into you on sidewalks, stand in line at the post office, weave through traffic, and act as if they are in a bubble—oblivious to their surroundings and gabbing away on a cell phone. In an article on eHow.com, Matthew Holohan wrote, "An epidemic of inconsiderate cell phone use has given the devices a bad reputation." You can do many things to avoid being a part of the epidemic. Consider these etiquette tips for cell-phone use.

- **Use your cell phone discreetly:** I think that most people agree that a telephone conversation should be private. Avoid carrying on cell-phone conversations in public places like restaurants, on sidewalks, while standing in line, and at the mall; it is considered rude by many people. When you must use your cell phone in public, do what you can to keep your voice volume down. Save your loud, emotional conversations for a phone booth or your home office.
- **Use your cell phone safely:** How often have you seen a cell-phone-equipped pedestrian wander into moving traffic? How often have you seen a cell-phone-equipped driver change lanes in front of you without looking? Driving while using a cell phone should be limited to emergencies, checking messages, and confirming directions—and then only when it is safe to do so. Until using the cell phone becomes completely hands-free with voice-activated dialing, it will not, in my humble opinion, be a safe activity while driving. Since cell phones can affect aircraft instrumentation, hospital equipment, and other sensitive instruments, use yours with plenty of discretion.
- **Use your cell phone sparingly:** I like to think of the cell phone as a tool for brief communication where no other means is available. Hundreds of free minutes seem to have given some people consent to be on the cell phone simply because there's no cost. Use your cell phone sparingly, both in frequency and in length, for proper public etiquette, for safety reasons, and maybe even for health reasons.
- **Call back on a land line when you're losing signal:** Cellular telephones, even the new PCS (personal communication system) and digital systems, have a long way to go before they can match the reliability and sound-quality standards of the plug-in-the-wall telephone. If you talk to frequent wireless users, you know the frustration of poor connections, dropped calls, noisy cells, interruptions by other cell phones, and weak batteries. Extend the courtesy of using a wired phone for lengthy, important discussions whenever you can.

- **Turn the phone off:** We've all heard ringing cell phones at conferences, restaurants, concerts, on public transportation, and even at church. Especially annoying to me are the phones that ring a chorus of Dixie or the owner's college fight song. Have the courtesy to turn off your cell phone (or put it in the vibrate mode if you have it) when you are in a place where others would be disturbed by a ringing phone. I know it's easy to forget, but don't let a deeply embarrassing moment make you commit it to habit. If your phone happens to ring at the wrong moment, don't make it worse by answering it. Quickly turn it off and apologize to those around you.

How bad have manners gotten? In late 1999, San Diego Mayor Susan Golding went so far as to ask movie and performing arts theater owners, local university presidents, and school superintendents to voluntarily join a cell phone courtesy campaign to limit cell-phone use in certain public places. The point is, you can and should have telecommuting success without annoying others.

Pager Etiquette

Much like cell phones, pagers can be valuable mobile tools. The more sophisticated pagers with instant messaging, e-mail, and Web access can provide the power telecommuter with flexibility, connectivity, and reachability. However, pagers can easily become annoying distractions. Many etiquette issues for cell phones apply to pagers, and without repeating the same rules, allow me to offer some suggestions unique to pagers.

- **If you don't need it, don't bring it:** Unlike your cell phone, which can be used in emergencies, your pager should be with you only when you are on call.
- **Turn it off:** Don't allow your pager to interrupt an important meeting or lunch with a client. Most systems have a delay feature that stores messages when your pager is off. If you don't have the delay feature, make sure that people who normally page you know the times you don't wish to be disturbed.

- **Establish some rules:** If a small group of people normally pages you, establish some rules about when a page is appropriate, the use of code words to express urgency, how quickly you will routinely respond, and when you expect to be unavailable. If callers know you will jump to a phone every time your pager goes off, you may be setting yourself up for needless pages, unnecessary interruptions, and control over your time.
- **Establish an escape plan:** If you are with other people and are expecting a critical page, sit at the end of a row or near an exit so you can excuse yourself to a private area or telephone.
- **Exercise common courtesy:** When you receive a page while in a meeting or carrying on a conversation, turn it off immediately and then allow others the courtesy of finishing their thoughts before looking at your pager. Politely ask to be excused if you must take action. Since some pagers can be heard by others in the vibrate mode, the sooner you turn it off, the better. Plus, don't leave your pager set to the vibrate mode on a conference table unless you want to cause people to jump when it starts bouncing on the table!

Irrespective of the technology you are using to communicate, proper etiquette is approximately 10 percent rules and 90 percent common sense. This holds especially true with conferencing. Give consideration to the following tips as you prepare for remote meetings.

Teleconference, Videoconference, and Online Conference Etiquette

The term *electronic meeting* refers to any formal interaction between a group of people separated by distance and facilitated by electronics. Effective use of electronic conferencing will continue to play an increasing role in your success as a power telecommuter. Today, with streaming video, high-speed connectivity, freely available software, and video cameras on many new computers, videoconferencing and online meetings are becoming more common as a standard communication option for telecommuters. There are three common types of electronic conferencing.

- **The teleconference:** When three or more people are connected live by telephone, they are on a *teleconference.* Even though basic teleconferencing and three-way calling have been used in business for over two decades, many users do not follow or perhaps do not know the etiquette rules. These rules become much more important as the number of teleconference participants increases.
- **The videoconference:** A *videoconference* is established when two or more people are connected live electronically and are able to see each other's image on a screen. Although the videoconference will not completely replace face-to-face meetings, it can add important visual cues to distance communication such as facial expressions, body language, and the ability to hold up an object for viewing.
- **The online conference:** The *online conference* has all of the benefits of a videoconference but with far more interactive features, all accomplished over the Internet. Universal access to the Internet and the availability of online meeting software (such as Microsoft's NetMeeting, Lotus's Sametime, and CUseeME Networks' MeetingPoint) is giving the online conference improved, accessible remote communication. The online conference offers new versatility with collaboration features. These features include a slide-show presentation, a whiteboard (which allows participants to make a sketch on screen that all participants can see), document editing (allowing users to change, highlight, add, or delete sections of a document that appears on everyone's screen), and application sharing (allowing all participants to use an application, such as a graphics program, without requiring that program to be installed on each user's computer).

One additional Web-enabled communication medium that deserves a mention is the *Web presentation.* Internet proliferation, commonly available presentation software (such as the RealPlayer from RealNetworks), and increased bandwidth have expanded the potential for audio and video presentations over the Internet. Just about any presentation that you have seen in person can now be presented live or played back online any time when set up properly. Web presentations, which are best suited for communication to mass audiences, are commonly used for new product introductions, paid professional seminars, shareholder meetings, and so on, further expanding your communication potential.

As the frequency of meetings and number of electronic conference participants and locations increase, the rules of etiquette become more important for maintaining control and communication effectiveness. I next review some ways you can maximize electronic conferences.

- **Conference set up:** As telecommuting increases, so will the opportunity for the power telecommuter to host electronic conferences. The ideal electronic conference host announces the meeting, sets the agenda, invites the participants, provides calling instructions, sets the meeting tone, maintains control, and provides a summary and list of action items if appropriate. Of course, when calling meetings, be sensitive to time zones.
- **Call a little in advance:** As a participant in an electronic conference, you will find that it is better to be a little early than a little late. I like to call five minutes in advance of teleconferences just in case there is some kind of trouble signing on. For online conferences and meetings, you may want to give yourself even more time in case you encounter software problems, connection delays, or network congestion.
- **Avoid distracting practices:** When participating in an electronic conference, make sure that you do not become the source of any distractions. Reduce background noise by turning off the radio, the television, or music. Find a way to prevent noise from an open window, a washing machine, or a neighbor's lawnmower from being heard. If your spouse, kids, or pets are in the house, make arrangements in advance to prevent interruptions. Also, use a speakerphone only if it has a mute button. Be sure to disable call waiting, don't use noisy cell phones, and excuse yourself if you absolutely must leave the conversation. If you have music-on-hold, set the receiver down. Otherwise the music will dominate the conversation, and you'll be the butt of jokes in the office for weeks.
- **Listen first, then talk:** Once again drawing from experience, I know it is fairly easy to appear foolish by asking a question that has been covered. Your credibility and professionalism as a telecommuter can be called into question if others perceive that you're not paying attention or asking questions just to get airtime.

- **Say your name each time you speak:** In large, interactive conferences or when many people are chiming in, it's important that the participants know who is speaking. In these situations, identify yourself before you make your point—especially if you haven't spoken in a while.
- **Don't interrupt or talk over others:** One way to immediately reduce your credibility and respect is to interrupt or talk over another speaker. Since modern conferencing systems have a feature that allows only one speaker at a time, usually no one can be heard when two people talk.

Electronic conferencing can be the telecommuter's best friend. In organizations where meetings are frequent, it should become standard practice for telecommuters to attend via speakerphone. Even though your attending meetings remotely may be met with resistance, the power telecommuter must remain persistent, professional, and adaptive to the needs of others so that telecommuting opposition is minimized. That's about it for etiquette. Next I review tips on when to use different media for different communication goals.

Choosing the Right Medium for Your Communication Goals

Do you ever consider how much influence the communication medium you choose has on the message's impact? What would you think of your manager if you were told that your annual performance review would be held by phone this year? How would it make you feel if someone for whom you have great respect sent you a handwritten thank-you note? How does it affect your working relationship when a coworker or client won't return your calls? As telecommuters become more mobile and expand their network of contacts internationally, selecting the appropriate communication media for the message becomes more important for telecommuting success.

In today's fast-paced, digital workplace it is tempting to use the communication medium for convenience, not for appropriateness. Saul Carliner, assistant professor in the information design programs at Bentley College in Waltham, Massachusetts, specializes in appropriate communication and offers these general guidelines:

Selecting the Correct Medium for the Best Communication

What Is the Purpose of Your Communication?	How Should It Be Communicated?
Kick off a project or plan with the team.	Face-to-face.
Hold a monthly project status meeting.	Face-to-face (preferred); video or online conference (next best); telephone conference (least preferred).
Acknowledge the birthday of a direct coworker or manager; send well wishes for serious illness or death in the family.	A timely greeting card signed by the workgroup (if none from the group, by you personally) left discreetly in the workplace or mailed to home.
Introduction to a new, critical member of the work team.	Welcome note by e-mail, then introductory telephone call to set up a face-to-face lunch meeting.
Return a signed agreement or contract.	On paper through the mail (first choice); if time sensitive use fax, followed with the hard copy by mail.
Request for an appointment with a busy executive.	Contact the administrative assistant and determine who sets the person's calendar and the preferred communication medium; then act accordingly.
Hold an important one-on-one meeting to persuade or gain support.	Face-to-face (preferred); telephone or online conference (next best).
Send a meeting reminder.	E-mail as well as (but not in place of) post to an Intranet site.
Distribute meeting minutes.	E-mail; after approval, post to an Intranet site.
Resolve a personal concern or problem.	Face-to-face. If the issue is not immediately resolved, continue meeting face-to-face and follow up by memo on internal stationery—do not use e-mail.

(continues)

(continued)

Selecting the Correct Medium for the Best Communication

What Is the Purpose of Your Communication?	How Should It Be Communicated?
Receive an annual performance review.	Face-to-face.
Get a coworker, prospect, or client to return your call after you have left two voice-mail messages.	Talk with an assistant or coworker to determine a possible reason and the best time to reach the person, then act accordingly. If just busy, try calling early or late in the day. Try another medium such as e-mail or fax to get the person's attention. If there's no interest, continued attempts could alienate the individual.
Follow up an e-mail request to which no response has been received.	After three days, a phone call. The person might be away. He or she is more likely to tell you in a phone message than in an e-mail.
Follow up a phone call or voice-mail request to which no response has been received.	Determine if the person is away and, if so, call on his or her return. If not, e-mail the message and ask for a response by a specific date.
Job interview.	Face-to-face (preferred); videoconference (alternative).
Accept a job offer.	Phone call, followed by formal letter on personal stationery.
International correspondence that will be occasional.	E-mail and occasionally by telephone if warranted.
International correspondence that will be ongoing.	If face-to-face meetings are not feasible, make at least one telephone contact. Then use e-mail or videoconferencing if available.
Add an individual to a postal or electronic mailing list.	Send a note asking permission. Once on the list, offer a way to opt out on subsequent correspondence.

Improving Communication Is an Ongoing Process

By now you have learned there is no substitute for good communication. If your basic communication skills need updating, update them. If you need to brush up on your communication etiquette, keep the tips in this chapter in mind and reread them every once in a while. To make your communication as effective as possible, be sure to use a medium that enhances the message.

Telecommuting success and staying in the loop can be complicated, but once you have your routine in place, it becomes, well, routine! One of the best ways to take your telecommuting potential to the next level is to make sure you fit in while you are working away from the office, which just happens to be the topic of the next chapter.

CHAPTER 7

Fitting in While Working Away

KEY CHAPTER POINTS

- It's time to solidify your telecommuting credibility.
- Ways to remain reachable without giving up quiet time.
- How to be part of a team while telecommuting.
- 10 tips for staying on the corporate radar screen.
- Tips from the pros on maintaining virtual relationships.
- How to handle your paper mail when working away from the main office.
- Making sure the boss knows what you're working on at home.
- Signs that it's time to visit the main office.

Developing and Maintaining Your Telecommuting Credibility

One of your biggest challenges as a telecommuter is remaining a visible, connected part of the organization while working away from the main office. The good news is that you can actually improve working relationships while working away. The bad news is that the odds of telecommuting success are typically stacked against you because it's not the norm, it's often resisted by managers and coworkers, and it takes hard work to do well. To beat these odds, you need to develop and maintain telecommuting credibility and the power telecommuter persona.

Telecommuters sometimes feel as if they have a target on their backs. In nearly every telecommuting organization I've seen, some people are just waiting for telecommuters to fail. These telecommuting skeptics will jump at the chance to play the "I told you telecommuting doesn't work" card. That's why fitting in while working away becomes critical.

So how do you fit in and strengthen relationships? First and foremost, you must establish your credibility through your professional telecommuter image. You must find ways to stay on the corporate radar, remain reachable without giving up quiet time, master virtual relationships, handle your paper mail, make sure the boss knows what you're doing at home and, finally, recognize signs that it's time to visit the main office.

By following the suggestions and tips in this chapter, your communication and interaction with others will become more focused, more considered, and more consistent.

If you make one behavior change as a telecommuter, it should be to establish your telecommuting credibility. To be taken seriously as a telecommuter, you must always be seen as a professional. Of course, you can and should have fun at the appropriate times. But if you leave any doubt whether you are working when at home, your telecommuting credibility can be nearly impossible to regain.

You should present your image as a telecommuting professional at the main office, with coworkers, with management, with clients and customers, and with family and friends. Consider these ideas on how to maintain a high credibility level as a telecommuter. Some of these suggestions are discussed in earlier chapters, but they are worth reiterating here.

- **Never joke about your telecommuting activity:** Consider the consequences of kidding about sleeping in or watching the baseball game on a telecommuting day. Telecommuting skeptics will use it as ammunition to question the credibility of your telecommuting activity. Always present your telecommuting experiences in a positive light. Regularly show evidence of the quantity and quality of work that you are producing as a result of your remote environment. See Chapter 2 for further discussion.
- **Keep your home office clean and organized:** Keeping things where you can find them is incredibly important. If you have difficulty finding information, after two or three such incidents your manager may lose confidence in you and in your working away from the main office. Your home office should remain clean and organized well enough to allow you to work efficiently.
- **Maintain a clear barrier from family activities:** It is your responsibility to prevent interruptions and distractions from family activities. As you know, a telecommuter cannot be the primary caretaker during work hours. If older children are in the home after school, make a house rule that when your office door is closed, you are not to be disturbed unless blood or fire is involved. It is critical that all family members take this rule seriously so that you can maintain the professionalism needed to carry out home work. See Chapter 5 for information on training family members to respect your work time at home.
- **Keep the volume low:** There is no harm in having talk radio, classical music, or the television on in the background while you work as long as it does not distract you. However, it may send the wrong message to callers if they can hear it in the background. Make sure the volume is turned down when you're on the phone with colleagues and clients.

- **Be sensitive to distracting background noises:** On a nice day, you can open the windows and enjoy outside air. At the same time, noises from kids, traffic, or the neighbor's dog could be distracting both to you and someone on the other end of the phone. Remember that these noises can seem amplified to a caller, sounding out of place for a business call and distracting on a conference call. Be ready to close the window or move to a quieter spot.
- **Reply to communication promptly:** Your coworkers' confidence in the effectiveness of telecommuting will erode rapidly if you seem to disappear on telecommuting days. Responses to e-mail, voice mail, and fax correspondence should be prompt and predictable. See the sample communication commitments later in the chapter.
- **Dress for success:** It will take many years for the telecommuting industry to rid itself of the "bunny slippers" image that originated from a television ad in the late nineties. Skeptical managers have trouble imagining workers accomplishing anything while dressed like that. However, unless you use videoconferencing, the clothing you wear (or don't wear) while working in your home office is a personal choice. Some people need to dress as if they are going to the main office. To others, it makes no difference. The key is to not allow your clothing to become an issue with your work. Dress comfortably for the season and your psychological needs.
- **Celebrate your return to the office:** When I was a product manager for a telecommunications manufacturer, I remember asking one of our brightest sales engineers how he could stand being on the road, away from home nearly every week. He told me it was actually healthy for him and his wife. He enjoyed traveling, visiting with his clients, and introducing products. Although he missed his wife, he was greeted with a reunion celebration each time he arrived home. My sales friend also made it a point to celebrate his return to the office. He would make the rounds, greet us with a joke, or tell us about his trip. After I was promoted into sales, I adopted this concept of celebration. Each time I arrived home after a trip, I made sure that I had something for my wife and daughter and made the rounds with my friends and colleagues at work. One way to stay in the loop *after* working away is to celebrate your return to the office in a similar way.

- **Establish some rules for when you are in the main office:** Once you are accustomed to working uninterrupted at home, attempting to work in the main office can become extra frustrating. Coworkers will want to chat, managers will need to discuss the latest projects, and the phone won't stop ringing. Team members at Sapient, an Internet strategy consulting company in Cambridge, Massachusetts, have instituted rules that let others know that they wish not to be disturbed. One rule might stipulate that if an engineer is wearing a baseball cap or has headphones on, he or she is concentrating on something that needs full attention. Whatever you do to send the "do not disturb" message, be sure not to overuse it lest your coworkers begin to believe that you are an unapproachable telecommuter.

The privilege of telecommuting comes with big responsibilities, and very few telecommuter traits are as important as maintaining credibility. Because it is an earned privilege, telecommuting can be taken away with the most innocent impropriety witnessed by the wrong person.

Establishing Availability Expectations and Making Communication Commitments

Establishing availability expectations and communication commitments are a sign of a power telecommuter. "Have an established schedule for checking voice mail and e-mail," said Phil Montero, founder of YouCanWorkFromAnywhere.com. Montero suggests that you let others know your schedule for checking your e-mail and voice mail while you're out of the office. "This promotes better communication and avoids any confusion about the timeliness of messages being delivered," he explained.

If you haven't done so, now would be the perfect time to clarify to your communication and reachability commitments with your manager, coworkers, and those with whom you are in regular contact. Here is sample correspondence you may wish to use as a model.

To my coworkers:

As you know, I have been telecommuting part-time for several months, and I appreciate your support. I have been able to accomplish my work goals more effectively and, I believe, have improved my contribution to the group and to the organization.

(continues)

(continued)

Since effective communication is critical to the success of continued telecommuting by me and others in the workgroup, I want to make sure that you are aware of the communication commitments that I made as a part of my telecommuting agreement and of the most effective way of reaching me when I am working at home.

When will I work at home? I expect to work one to two days per week at home on an as-needed basis, especially when an assignment requires large blocks of uninterrupted time or as a project deadline warrants. I will negotiate a telecommuting day with my manager, work in my home office, and then review the work on my return.

How will you reach me? Each telecommuting day I will change my voice-mail greeting to say whether I am working in the main office or away. I will check my voice mail and e-mail regularly, so please leave me a message. If it is critical that you reach me right away, do not hesitate to contact me at the number below or through my manager. As part of my telecommuting commitment, I have established the following communication and meeting routines:

I will check e-mail at 8 a.m., noon, and 5 p.m. each day.

I will check voice mail at 8 a.m., noon, and 5 p.m. each day.

I plan to always attend the Monday staff meetings and bimonthly product review meetings.

For meetings called while I am telecommuting, I will attend by speaker-phone, or when necessary, in person.

To reach me in an emergency, please call 202-555-2397. Suzy Floyd has agreed to act as my office-based telecommute contact, so if you need to reach me right away, Suzy or my manager will likely know how.

Thanks again for your support. Please let me know if you have any questions.

Sincerely,

Mary Telecommuter

Remaining Reachable Without Giving Up Quiet Time

As I've said repeatedly, a key telecommuting benefit is quiet, uninterrupted time in the home office. However, power telecommuters by nature want to be highly interactive and regularly accessible. The paradox here is remaining reasonably reachable without giving up that precious quiet time. Here are a few options and tips I would like you to consider.

- **Remain reachable while telecommuting:** Establish and keep your reachability and communication commitments. If you are developing telecommuting trust with your manager, make an effort to be available for those random "checking on you" calls until a routine feels appropriate. Of course, there's no way to be available 100 percent of the time, so state in your voice-mail recording that you will get back to the caller within an hour or some reasonable time.
- **Remain reachable while on the move:** If you wish to be found wherever you are at any moment, there is a way to do it. The question is, how reachable do you need to be while traveling? Only you can answer that. The answer lies in the ideal mix of business need, privacy, productivity, safety, etiquette, cost, and practicality.
- **Become a transparent telecommuter:** The term *transparent telecommuting* applies when individuals work in a remote location, but their work location remains irrelevant or unknown to those with whom they interface. These workers are as accessible, and sometimes even more accessible, than they were in the main office. They frequently have access to all the on-screen information from the main office. One of my first clients moved a dozen individuals to their homes as transparent telecommuters. After a thorough evaluation of their communication needs and patterns, each was provided a cell phone and pager and was instructed on effective voice-mail use. When someone calls the regular office number, it first rings in the home office. If the employee is not there, the call is forwarded to wherever the individual happens to be. If while at home the individual needs to work uninterrupted, calls can be forwarded to voice mail and retrieved later. The department has been complimented on

how much more available the workers have become. Many people to this day have no idea that this group had all moved home to work.

The Home Agent: The Ultimate Transparent Telecommuter

My favorite transparent telecommuter example is the full-time home agent (airline reservation agent or insurance customer service agent, for example) who works from a fully equipped, permanent home office. To the customer, the agent is in a call center. One organization even provided call center background noise for home agents because the "silence" was noticeable to customers.

Computing and communications technology emulates all functions of the main office remotely, including data transfer, supervisory monitoring, and online work activity tabulation. When a customer calls, there is no reason to believe the agent is anywhere but in a call center with other agents. If the agent needs to get caught up on paperwork or stops to take a lunch break, the system puts the employee on standby, and calls are directed to other agents.

Large organizations with home agents quickly discover the benefits. Office overhead is reduced, productivity increases, agents can be anywhere in the world, agents can be immediately available during unexpected call volume, agents don't need to commute during late night and early morning hours, and agents can go off the clock during slow periods when call volume decreases.

As you can see, there are ways of remaining reachable without giving up quiet time. As a quick review, remember these tips for staying reachable:

- Commit to being available during specific core hours, allowing a balance of quiet time and accessibility.
- Make an effort to be available for those random "checking on you" calls.
- Have at least two and ideally three ways of being reached in case of a technology failure.

- Make sure your regular contacts know your routine for checking messages.
- In your voice-mail recording, indicate how quickly you will normally return calls.
- Provide an emergency number to your manager and perhaps one coworker.

Using these tips and the other suggestions in this book will go a long way in keeping you in touch with the office. But what about teamwork? Won't it be difficult to remain a viable, productive member of a work team while telecommuting? It may be a little easier than you think.

Teamwork, Telecommuting, and Playing Your Part

At first glance, teamwork and telecommuting appear to be at opposite poles of the universe. The question frequently asked by skeptical managers is "How can you have a team with a dispersed workforce?" The truth is, telecommuting can enhance the effectiveness of teamwork by helping everyone clearly focus on organizational goals. As a telecommuter, you need to make an extra effort to remain a contributing, valuable team member.

To many people, teamwork implies face-to-face interactivity of individuals from a variety of departments who provide their expertise toward a project's completion. The fallacy is the face-to-face part. If you analyze team interaction, the time the team spends together is minimal. Project meetings are a primary element in moving projects forward, but most of the team members' time is spent working on the project independent of teammates. As a telecommuter, your value will not be diminished because you work from home—unless you allow it.

As a member of various teams within and outside your organization, you have certain responsibilities. You must remain aware of team and project goals, schedules, changes, and obstacles. You are expected to keep your commitments, participate in meetings, and make a specific contribution to the process. As a mobile member of the team, some these challenges can be magnified, especially if telecommuting is not fully accepted by the team members.

As a power telecommuter, you must be extra vigilant in communicating well with your teammates, in being sensitive to concerns or hidden animosity they may have about telecommuting, and in being flexible by attending meetings you could just as well attend by speakerphone. In team situations, it is especially important to remain aware that your telecommuting credibility is always on the line. Word about sleeping late, missing your deadlines, or playing golf one afternoon can travel fast among those who take pleasure in proving that telecommuting doesn't work.

The Virtual Team Can Work Very Well

Virtual teams can work, and under the proper circumstances, they can work very well. A small sales organization at Arthur Andersen has been operating as a virtual team for several years. The sales team director believes in it—he lives in Montana. He and the other seven team members work predominantly from their homes in different parts of the country and get together at regular, very specific times each week by teleconference.

"There is absolutely no doubt that much more is accomplished in this format than in face-to-face meetings," said Paul Rukenbrod, another manager on the team. Why? Because the meetings cover very specific agenda items, start and end on time, and stick to the business at hand. "There's not much chit-chat during the meetings," he said. "There's kind of an unwritten rule that small talk happens as people are joining the call, but once the meeting starts, it's all business."

Another rule is that virtual attendance is mandatory. If for some reason you are absolutely unable to participate, you're expected to let someone know. Since team members have access to one another's calendars, they all know if a teammate has an appointment immediately after the call and will be sure to end the meeting promptly. One in ten meetings involve online document sharing. The others are pure teleconference.

Why does the virtual meeting format work so well? Rukenbrod, who helps his clients rediscover the underutilized potential of sales calls by phone, believes that virtual meetings, given the appropriate meeting management and disciplines, can be more effective than traditional face-to-face meetings because

- In face-to-face meetings people tend to be late. When meetings are on the phone, you tend to make it a priority and respect the time of others. "For the convenience of not having to travel to the meeting, the least I can do is be on time," he said.
- Virtual teams tend to communicate better. Body language is not that important with this team since they know each other so well. Regular virtual meetings increase your awareness of audible cues that you would miss in person.
- The meetings have very specific objectives, and everyone knows exactly what is expected of them in advance.

Making the transition to the virtual meeting format can be tough. "As people move away from face-to-face, it's sometimes difficult to break away from this traditional meeting process," said Rukenbrod. "But eventually, there is a revelation among the group that virtual is the best way." Admitting this format is not suited for everybody, he said that this group would probably have difficulty operating any other way.

Alexandria, Virginia–based Rukenbrod, who commutes to the Washington, D.C., office one day a week to "put in an appearance," said the team gets together once a quarter for a lunch or breakfast meeting.

"We're firm believers in the virtual team," stated Ruckenbrod, and he offers no excuse for the team not performing. "If the group is not meeting its objectives, it's not likely that the method of meeting is the problem." It's pretty obvious that the virtual team model works, and it works well for this organization. The power telecommuter can play a role in the success of virtual teams by consistently following the rules, meeting objectives and expectations, and helping others feel at ease in the nontraditional meeting format.

10 Ways to Stay on the Corporate Radar Screen

The office can be an awful place to work, but it has distinct advantages. A chance meeting in the hall with a project team leader or bumping into an executive in the cafeteria can solve a major problem or create consideration for promotion. These unplanned encounters play a positive role in effective employee communication and individual interaction.

In a telecommuting situation, opportunities for chance meetings, lunchtime discussions, and a quick project chat during a walk through the hall are diminished. The "out of sight—out of mind" adage can become a reality if you are not careful. There are, however, ways that you can supplement these lost opportunities and stay on the corporate radar screen.

1. **Make regular first contact:** I learned a long time ago there are significant advantages to making regular first contacts with clients, managers, teammates, and anyone else with whom I am working. This means instead of *them calling you* for a project update, a follow-up discussion on a major change in direction, or a progress report on a delayed request for information, *you should call them*. Being proactive shows you have others' best interest in mind. Besides, it's much easier to deal with problems before they reach crisis proportions. If you make regular "just checking in" calls with your first-line contacts, you will be in a much better position to deal with situations before they escalate into a crisis, and you will reduce the potential of earning a disappearing telecommuter perception.
2. **Invite key people to see your home office:** It's human nature to draw conclusions without visual cues. A skeptical manager's negative image of your home office, for instance, could act as a constant anchor that slows your internal progress. Consider inviting that skeptical manager over for a meeting or a quick lunch. A positive experience may change this person's perspective about what it takes to work at home.
3. **Build a team of supporters:** Many people in your organization may be telecommuting supporters, and it's always a good idea to have them in your camp in case something hits the fan. Seek them out and establish relationships with them. Some organizations with mature programs have a telecommuting steering committee to monitor and solve problems, to keep telecommuting on the minds of employees through a newsletter, to assure fairness in the policy and procedures, and to present telecommuting positively to upper

management. You may want to consider getting involved with such an activity if you believe it can help your cause.

4. **Make yourself very visible when in the office:** When you visit the main office, don't schedule large blocks of time holed up in an office or conference room. Keep a list of people who regularly assist you in your daily processes and make it a point to visit them. This may include people in the mailroom, shipping department, payroll, credit union, purchasing, engineering, manufacturing, and even the executive offices. If you regularly and personally remind people how important they are to you, they will respond with appreciation and support when you need them.

"Fitting in while working away wasn't much of a problem for technology folks in the old workplace because they were the only ones off-site! Now that a wide spectrum of employees and peers are working remote, technology people are having to learn new ways of relating, project managing, and keeping their visibility in an increasingly mobile environment."

Theresa Perry, president of Atlantek Network,
a recruiting firm specializing in high-tech placements

---

5. **Establish cross-functional relationships in the organization:** Networking outside your regular circle of contacts is more important as your telecommuting increases. There are plenty of activities that would connect you with others in your organization, such as taking employer-sponsored courses, volunteering for the organization's favorite charity, becoming a credit union board member, playing on the organization's golf, tennis, or bowling league, or helping with the annual picnic. The next time a new position is created in a department outside your own, one of these relationships could mean the difference between your being considered for it or not.
6. **Bring a mentor into your life:** To this day I am thankful to the handful of people who took me under their wing in various stages of my career. As a telecommuter, it is so important to have someone pulling for you back at the main office. Well-placed mentors can introduce you to the right people, nominate you for an important

project team, keep you informed on organizational directions, influence an executive decision in your favor, and provide counsel for challenges and tough decisions. When the opportunity presents itself, be sure to become a mentor yourself so you can help others.

7. **Attend important meetings:** Sometimes your absence from an important gathering can say more to management than being there with a stellar presentation. You simply can't attend all meetings, so choose them wisely and make the best of them when you do. Will there be opportunities to network with key individuals before or after the meeting? Will top executives attend? Has it been a long time since you have attended in person? The answer to these and other questions will help you decide whether to attend.
8. **Maintain relationships with well-placed people:** Staying in the loop while working away involves staying on the radar screen of others. This may be dipping a little deep into the political cauldron, but politics—albeit sometimes detrimental—is a common part of any organization. Make it a point to stay in contact and even visit key individuals in the organization who are outside your reporting structure. These people might include an executive assistant, the information technology director, the human resources director, and the shipping manager. These people can be influential in helping you with a computer problem, getting an appointment with an executive, expediting a package for a customer, or helping with other challenges you may face.
9. **Stay in the spotlight:** Good news about your telecommuting travels fast and can be excellent public relations exposure for you and your organization. These days, newspaper and television reporters are hungry for good examples of people working from home. If you wish to seek publicity, make yourself available to the media (don't forget your organization's newsletter!). Next time you see an article in a magazine or newspaper on telecommuting, for instance, send a note to the reporter or letter to the editor expressing your support for the concept and add your experiences. Chances are that you will receive a return contact and maybe get on their contact list. Before you make your media debut, however, be sure to review your organization's media guidelines so that you don't step on internal toes. Finally, please don't allow photos of you in your home office

with children or pets. These images say a thousand words that you don't want to say.

10. **Establish a good relationship with a main office buddy:** You will read this more than once in this book because it's important. As your time in the main office decreases, the more things you may miss. Establish an agreement with someone who you can trust to regularly keep you informed on office changes, rumors, announcements, and other activities that could be of interest to you. It can be extremely useful to have someone keep you in the office information loop so that you can react appropriately.

Finding ways to stay on the corporate radar screen is one of the most important investments you can make as a telecommuter. It's highly complementary to efforts in maintaining virtual relationships. Let's take a look at some tips from the pros on virtual relationships.

Tips from the Pros on Maintaining Virtual Relationships

Maintaining virtual relationships can be difficult, but it's absolutely necessary for the power telecommuter. It's hard enough to keep a normal relationship going, much less one in which you see someone three or four times a month, or three or four times a year. To gain insight on this challenging topic, I asked several experts in various fields what it takes to maintain a productive virtual relationship. Here's what they had to say.

- **Remain available to others:** "Be available to coworkers, customers, and other colleagues during traditional office hours," suggested Emory Mulling, chairman of the Mulling Companies. Mulling, who has been active in career guidance and training since 1973, pointed out that one advantage of working from home is that you can return voice-mail and e-mail messages any time of the day or night. "However," he warned, "if you are not accessible during normal office hours, you may inadvertently stall projects or frustrate coworkers."
- **Stay connected with your work and with others through technology:** "The concept of one assigned place to work, be it home or

corporate office, is dead," said John Vivadelli, president of Agilquest, a provider of hoteling reservations systems. "Mobility demands a network of shared, interconnected workplaces available whenever, wherever you need to work and accessible as easily as a reservation for air, car, or hotel. Work at home, walk to a telework center, subway to a downtown office, fly to a serviced business center—the new workplace is a workplace network." No matter where you connect, use the opportunity to stay in close contact with your managers, coworkers, and clients.

- **The more things change, the more they seem to stay the same:** "Virtual relationships are not really all that new," said Gail Martin, executive director of the International Telework Association & Council. "When you consider all the handwritten correspondence that passed between people since the delivery of mail began, most people rarely met in person if at all, and it often took months to receive the correspondence," she explained. "Today's virtual relationships are markedly different only by the speed and accessibility of technology, but they require the same attention, accuracy, and courtesies speeded up into real time."
- **Remain aware of time elapsed between communication:** Whether relating to a team member, supervisor, or employee, monitor the time between messages and initiate contact every so often even if it is for a check-in with no real substantive content," suggested Walter Siembab, principal with Siembab Planning Associates. "People tend to think the worst when contact is infrequent. Don't let that happen."
- **Make the effort to meet face-to-face:** "Informal time together helps maintain rapport and partly makes up for the casual exchanges that used to take place around the coffeepot," stated Joanne Pratt, a long-time telecommuting professional with Joanne H. Pratt Associates. Pratt recommended scheduling brown-bag lunches to give members of a workgroup relaxed time to bring up and solve problems.
- **The agony of poor connectivity lingers long after the joy of low cost:** "Dependable, secure, and fast connectivity with your coworkers and customers is as important as air," said Dean Brown, presi-

dent of Star Valley Communications, a communications consulting and marketing firm specializing in remote work. "Without it, life as a telecommuter is short." Brown recommended that before selecting your remote-access service, give careful consideration to your workflow, including your voice, fax, and data communications requirements. "Don't allow the allure of low-cost Internet access be your primary selection criteria," he warned. "Get to know the key attributes of the popular access services (ISDN, DSL, cable, and so on) so that you can make the best decision."

- **Keep several communication options available:** "Successful telecommuting requires not only good, open communication, but it is important to have several communication options available those who need to have access to you," explained Kristin Hunicke, public information specialist for the Georgia Clean Air Force, the state's vehicle emission inspection and maintenance program. Hunicke telecommutes one day a week and finds herself "being productive and getting projects done at home."
- **The secret to true remote work success:** "Two basic tools integrate you into your enterprise: The office building still has proper uses and the new 'virtual presence' technologies have theirs," explained telework consultant Stan Thompson. "True telework success consists in choosing between these tools instinctively, dynamically, correctly."
- **Be proactive in your communication:** "Before your managers ask or wonder what you're doing at home (and they will) leave a brief voice message each day outlining today's work plans and results from the previous day," said Frank Boyd, senior corporate relations coordinator for Georgia Power. Boyd, who started the company's telework program in 1992, also believes it is critical that you meet face-to-face with your manager regularly. "Schedule an hour for a meeting with your manager every two to four weeks to discuss business in greater detail," he suggested.
- **Make sure your presence is felt:** "Find new ways to become a virtual extravert, having your presence felt daily by your supervisor, co-workers, customers, and other stakeholders," said Warren Master, director of public management consulting at Clifton Gunderson.

- **Maintain good personal connections with colleagues:** "Staying connected with your boss and peers is extra important when you are not visible in the office every day like your coworkers," said Dr. Linda Kammire Tiffan, managing director of the HR Solutions Atlanta branch. Dr. Tiffan reminds telecommuters to consider how much information gets shared during random meetings at the coffee station, in the hallway, and in the rest room. "Take the time to send a quick e-mail or make a brief phone call to your colleagues and initiate a dialogue about current events, their children, outside interests, and the latest developments at work," she suggested. "Strong business relationships are important to your career success, and they are furthered as much by the good personal connections you make as by the quality of work that you perform. This may be more difficult to do when telecommuting, but it is well worth the effort."
- **If you're out of sight, don't stay out of mind:** "When your absence is being felt, make sure you're not forgotten," advised Eddie Caine, professional services manager for TManage. "Provide your supervisors and coworkers work updates and follow up with both verbal and written messages."

As you can see, you can take many approaches to establishing and maintaining virtual relationships. I hope these insights have helped broaden the possibilities for you. My next topic is often neglected by telecommuters until there's a crisis. I hope this discussion will stimulate you into establishing an effective system for handling paper and mail as a telecommuter.

Handling Paper and Mail As a Telecommuter

Have you thought about how you arrange for timely receipt of paper mail? Even though much of your correspondence is electronic, the pessimist in me says that important memos, reports, proposals, and other documents are bound to arrive at your main office in-box on the day you are telecommuting.

Having access to paper-based documents, publications, and materials when you need them can be a challenge for the frequent telecommuter. You can do a variety of things to organize, track, and have ready access to these materials. Of course, all of this depends on your telecommuting frequency and the importance of the information, but consider these tips for handling paperwork and mail as a telecommuter.

- **Have general mail forwarded:** You may want to have magazine and newsletter subscriptions, product announcements, and other general mail sent directly to your home office. Important mail, however, should be sent to the location at which you spend most of your work time.
- **Make an agreement with a mail screener:** Important announcements, airline tickets, software upgrades, security codes, and the occasional bouquet of flowers are bound to be delivered to your main office desk. Somehow you will need to be notified and arrangements made for you to receive them. Give consideration to making such arrangements with someone from the mailroom, someone who sorts and distributes the mail for the workgroup, or perhaps a nontelecommuting coworker. Whoever you choose, this is someone who must remain on your holiday gift list.
- **Keep a remote work satchel:** As I suggest elsewhere in the book, each time you leave the main office you should have the files, data, reference materials, contact information, and other critical work items you will need for a given task. If you plan this right, you won't need to duplicate each file or drive to the office because you forgot something. The power telecommuter carries a remote work satchel that is regularly purged and always available at home when needed.
- **Have a plan for outbound mail from your home office:** As a telecommuter, you will likely have the need to send letters or packages from your home office. For postal services, if traveling to the post office is inconvenient, you can leave outgoing mail with your postal carrier. The post office will provide you with an envelope to pay for postage if you need it. For overnight service, the most convenient method is to bring home overnight carrier envelopes, use the preprinted labels from your organization, and call the carrier for pickup.

Handling paper mail is frequently overlooked but not that difficult as a telecommuter. Another important element of telecommuting communication is keeping in close contact with your boss. Next I review a few things you can do to stay in that important loop.

Making Sure the Boss Knows What You're Doing at Home

In all of your telecommuting activity, there is no more important need than to stay in close communication with your immediate manager. This is as critical to telecommuting as breathing is to life.

Positioning yourself as a power telecommuter in the eyes of your manager will make your telecommuting life much easier. Although I've touched on many of these issues in previous chapters, they are important enough to summarize here:

- Establish and maintain your telecommuting credibility.
- Stay on the boss's radar screen.
- Become highly competent at "virtual relationships."
- Be proactive in your communication.
- Make frequent reality checks.
- Don't sabotage your telecommuting situation.

As I've said before, in the eyes of your manager, you will best fit in while working away by agreeing on your work before you leave for home, staying in touch while you're gone, tracking your progress, keeping excellent records, and being prepared to give the right answers to challenging questions. How does the power telecommuter do this? A day of telecommuting is not much different than traveling for business:

- You decide to travel and agree on trip objectives with your manager.
- You perform your traveling business.
- While traveling, you check e-mail and voice mail at the beginning, middle, and end of the day. As necessary, you contact your manager or coworkers.

- On return, you review accomplishments with your manager.

The power telecommuter uses a similar routine for remote work. This communication strategy prevents you from "disappearing."

What can you can do to keep the boss from wondering what you're doing while you are at home? Refer back to Chapter 2 and these tools:

- Mobile Work Task Identification Form
- Weekly Telecommuter Task and Activity Form
- Monthly Remote Work Activity Form

That's how you'll stay in the loop with your boss. If you telecommute mostly from home, watch for warning signs that it's time to increase your frequency of main office visits. I discuss these signs in the next section.

Signs That You Should Work at the Main Office More Frequently

Telecommuting is a great workplace alternative. If you're not careful, however, spending too much time in your telecommuting world can inadvertently turn you into a telehermit, causing you to become disconnected from important activities and events.

You must remain aware of the telehermit symptoms. It is absolutely critical for any telecommuter to watch for signs that it's time to visit and work at the main office more often. Some of these signs are subtle, and some are easy to miss. You may be out of the loop if

- **Your primary internal contacts have no time for you:** If it takes unusually long for your primary contacts to return your messages, or they don't seem to have time for you, make an appointment to visit with them as soon as possible to reestablish communication.
- **Your main office desk is regularly pilfered:** In an office situation where someone is gone more than he or she is in the office, it is not

unusual for coworkers to begin thinking of this individual as separate from the team. If this starts happening to you, use the tips in this chapter to remain more visible to your coworkers. If the situation continues, you may have to spend more time in the office.

- **You find yourself mastering creative work avoidance:** Telecommuting requires significant discipline, and, without someone watching you during the day, it can be tempting to spend time on nonwork activities. When I feel sluggish or unmotivated while working at home, I find myself giving in to an interesting old movie, searching for my name on the Web, or taking a nap in the afternoon. If you find yourself becoming a master at creative work avoidance at home, it's either time to spend more time in the office or time to make specific, ambitious workday commitments to your manager.
- **You have taken on an excessive workload:** It is far more common for a telecommuter to overwork than to underwork. If you find yourself taking on more work than you can handle or are constantly overcommitted, it may be a sign that you are overcompensating for the telecommuting privilege, attempting to prove that you are worthy. I can tell you from experience that the more work you volunteer to do, the more work you'll be volunteered to do by others. Take a serious look at your work activities as they relate to your job description and commitments. You may find that certain tasks are not helping you to achieve your committed objectives. To solve this, review your workload with your manager and come to an agreement on priorities. Your goal should be to do an excellent job on the work that is important.
- **Meetings are being held without you:** When you begin seeing the minutes to meetings to which you should have been invited, it's a good sign that you are falling off the organization's radar screen. Find your way back on the distribution list by expressing your interest to the meeting host, offering to make presentations or some contribution, or making an effort to attend these meetings in person until you become once again recognized as a major player.
- **You are last to get the software and equipment upgrades:** As your telecommuting lifeline, your remote computer and communication systems must always be compatible with the organization's systems.

A sure sign that it's time to increase your visibility is when you find yourself last on the upgrade list. If so, this is a good time to establish a relationship with the information technology manager or someone on staff who is responsible for upgrades. Find out how these upgrades are scheduled and if there is anything you can do to make the job of upgrading remote equipment easier.

- **You are not invited to social gatherings:** Staying in the loop at work includes participating in social gatherings like birthday and anniversary celebrations and after-work get-togethers. Although these gatherings may not be critical to your work, participating in them keeps you in the loop. To be included, pay a visit to the individuals in charge of these events next time you're in the office. Let this person know of your interest in participating, and volunteer to help in some way.
- **You are passed by for a promotion:** One downside of telecommuting is that reduced physical presence can give nontelecommuter job candidates a bit of an edge. Since telecommuting is probably just one of the reasons you are passed by for a promotion, you'll need to do a little investigating to find out *all* of the reasons. If not being in the office was a primary cause and being considered for other jobs is important you, you will need to either follow the "stay in the loop" recommendations throughout this book or telecommute less.

Look at each of these situations as a wake-up call to motivate you into action. Rather than taking self-pity or revenge, treat these signs as symptoms of a bigger problem. Try to analyze what's really causing the problem, discuss it openly with your manager or those involved, and begin immediately on a solution. Most important, make it clear that continued telecommuting will depend on bringing performance levels back up to *your* expectations.

I hope these ideas, tips, and suggestions have helped you develop a solid plan as you advance as a power telecommuter. Speaking of advancing, how can you be sure that you will continue to be successful as a telecommuter? How will you improve your chances of long-term success? How can you be assured of excellent performance reviews? What about a retirement strategy? These are some of the questions I review and answer in the next chapter.

CHAPTER 8

Positioning Yourself for the Future

KEY CHAPTER POINTS

- You can always be a better telecommuter.
- How to regularly earn excellent or superior performance evaluations as a telecommuter.
- New ways to prepare yourself for future opportunities.
- Consider these telecommuter career path strategies that work.
- Tips for finding a telecommuting job.
- What the Web sites offering home-based jobs won't tell you.
- It's not too early to think about retirement strategies.
- Making the most of your telecommuting privilege.

No Matter How Good You Are, You Can Always Telecommute Better

Whether you are hoping to be a telecommuter, are just getting started, or have been doing it for a while, you can prepare yourself to telecommute better in the months and years to come. Before discussing how to position yourself for the future, however, perhaps it would be useful to review the key points of the previous chapters.

- **Chapter 1. Working in the new workplace presents new challenges:** You know the workplace is very different from just a generation ago and that it requires a whole new worker. Since telecommuting is a byproduct *and* a catalyst of this new workplace, there has never been a better time to be a telecommuter.
- **Chapter 2. Positioning yourself as a power telecommuter is critical:** It takes a lot of work to become a telecommuter. There are plenty of benefits, yet many pitfalls and traps can sabotage your telecommuting privilege. Raising your telecommuting persona to power telecommuter will help you overcome these obstacles, earn credibility, command respect, and achieve success.
- **Chapter 3. Maximizing contemporary technology tools is essential:** Successful telecommuters must be proficient with the technology rules and tools that apply to their situation, recognizing that technology boils down to platforms, bottlenecks, needs, and options. The power telecommuter can become proficient at technology without becoming a technology geek but must know enough to avoid technology gaps and disasters. To stay successful, you must maximize your present technology investment and future technology position.
- **Chapter 4. Making the most of your home office must be a priority:** In creating an ideal home office, it helps to establish a list of goals, projects, and acquisitions to plan for equipment and supplies. You must decide what you need and what you don't, create a layout of your ideal space, and maintain a safe, secure area. You must also understand the insurance needs and tax implications of a home office.

- **Chapter 5. Creating the ideal telecommuting environment is critical for success:** The power telecommuter must practice proactive productivity habits and be sure that everyone knows and respects your telecommuting rules. In an ideal environment, the telecommuter is an excellent time manager, relies on others to help accomplish remote work goals, and strikes a delicate balance between work, family, and personal time.
- **Chapter 6. There is no substitute for good communication:** The power telecommuter first must brush up on basic communication skills and then learn, practice, and master the etiquette of today's technology tools. You must also know when to use the correct communication medium.
- **Chapter 7. You must work hard to fit in while working at home:** As a telecommuter, you must first establish credibility and then maintain it by remaining reachable, staying on the corporate radar screen, building effective virtual relationships, handling paper mail, and making sure the boss knows what you accomplish at home. Finally, the power telecommuter must act on signs that it's time to visit the main office.

You're now at the final chapter—positioning yourself for your telecommuting future. As you discovered in previous chapters and perhaps in real life, this is no easy task. To position yourself for the telecommuting future, you must first look at the rapidly changing job environment and decide where you will fit in. You must wake up each morning ready to take on the telecommuting day, being well prepared with a telecommuting mind-set and a remote work discipline whether you are telecommuting that day or not.

Your telecommuting future is driven by your daily actions and routines, by how you position yourself for short-term success, and finally, by the planning decisions you make that will govern your career direction. You will regularly position yourself to earn the highest performance ratings you can. At the same time, you will want to look ahead, scanning the horizon for opportunities, positioning yourself for new career path options, and possibly searching for a new, challenging position that offers a telecommuting option.

You may find yourself taking on the challenge of becoming a free agent, otherwise known as an independent contractor. Perhaps you'll develop a retirement strategy, using your telecommuting experience as a building block for a new job or activity past standard retirement age. To do any or all of this, you need to take all the knowledge you have gained to make the most of your telecommuting privilege and then clear a path for long-term telecommuting success by making a commitment to prepare well every day for your telecommuting experience. Let's begin by reviewing some ways you can maintain an excellent or superior performance rating as a telecommuter.

Tips for Earning Excellent or Superior Performance Evaluations

Remote workers must work a little harder to show peers they are pulling their workload weight, especially where telecommuting is new or the manager is not fully supportive. To earn and maintain excellent or superior performance evaluations first implies that you regularly meet your manager's expectations. That given, you need to stay visible to the boss, develop a skill for establishing work expectations with your manager, track and report on your work activities, and solicit a regular performance status review.

Remaining "Visible" Is a Must

One concern of even the best telecommuters is the effects of an "out of sight, out of mind" syndrome: When out of the office, advancement and recognition opportunities are reduced. Telecommuting can be detrimental to your future, but it doesn't have to be. With some thoughtful planning and deliberate communication, telecommuting can enhance your potential for visibility because you communicate frequently and clearly and accomplish projects in a focused way. Give consideration to the following ideas, some of which I discuss earlier in a different context:

- **Develop a rapport with your manager:** As you know, remote work typically requires more dialogue between the manager and the telecommuter for establishing work objectives and evaluating the results. In establishing a good rapport with your manager, your goal should be to have an open and regular dialogue, to volunteer information before it is requested, and to constantly receive feedback on expectations.

- **Be there when it makes sense:** Being present in certain work situations is critical for staying aware of office politics, for getting executive exposure, and especially for attending meetings and activities deemed important by your manager. Remain aware of such opportunities and demands, and schedule face-time accordingly.
- **Remain reachable:** Check your e-mail and voice mail at regular times during the day and consistently respond within a reasonable time, say, within 2 to 3 hours, but no longer than 24 hours. Those attempting to reach you should never be given the impression that telecommuting is making it more difficult to reach you than before.
- **Manage your telecommuting image:** To be taken seriously as a telecommuter, it is important to build a professional image and never make light of telecommuting. Talking about the results of a day baseball game, playing loud music in the background, or being consistently unavailable can cause doubt on the legitimacy of your telecommuting.
- **Establish a main office buddy:** There will always be surprise changes, announcements, crises, and rumors in an office environment. The power telecommuter stays in the loop by depending on a coworker to convey such news as it occurs.

You and Your Manager Must Remain on the Same Page

Your lack of proximity can increase the potential for work tasks to miss the mark. To prevent this from happening, you must first understand and then execute the work instructions as your manager expects. Because a work task is often negotiated and modified as it is being assigned, it is critical that both parties are always on the same page. Consider these tips.

- **Look at the big picture:** Knowing how your work fits in the larger scheme of things assures that it will also fit when it's done. Have your manager clearly explain this perspective.

- **Agree on the particulars:** Make sure that you agree with your manager on such elements as time to complete, where the work will be performed, the budget and tools required, periodic reporting expectations, and details on the delivery of the final work output.
- **Master the art of establishing work expectations:** Have you ever turned in a work assignment that you thought was some of your best work, only to have your manager tell you that it was done incorrectly? Even the best workers and managers make assumptions about work output expectations without proper confirmation.
- **Keep good notes:** It bears repeating that good records of your telecommuting activities are critical. It's a good idea to summarize assignment instructions, correspondence, and work task milestones so that you can refer to these notes when needed. For complicated assignments, you may even want to share your summary of the assignment.
- **Repeat task instructions as you get them:** At the conclusion of work task discussions, summarize the changes verbally and follow up with a quick e-mail summary. Since it is likely that your task goals and instruction details will change, get into the habit of repeating the assignment verbally and in writing.
- **Send a test sample:** If you are developing a lengthy paper or computer program, why not send an early sample to your manager to assure that you are on the right track?
- **Perform regular reality checks:** On large or complicated tasks, confirm the work direction at regular intervals to assure that you are handling the project properly. A small course correction early in the process can save huge embarrassment later.
- **Accurately track and report your activities:** As discussed earlier, you will likely need to track your activities more closely than non-telecommuting coworkers. Your boss should never have to ask, "What did you do when you worked at home last Tuesday" because your end-of-the-week report was on his or her desk on Friday. Your records should be so good that if anyone asked you what you accomplished on Tuesday—any Tuesday—you would be able to tell

him or her. This "burden of proof" is good practice and causes telecommuters to be much more responsible for their workday.

- **Solicit a regular performance review:** When I was in the corporate world over 10 years ago, it was fairly customary to receive a performance review once a year. During the rest of the year, the only clue I had about my performance was when I dipped below my numbers or fell behind on a project. If things are pretty much the same for you today, it is up to you to put some kind of mechanism in place for regular feedback. Whether it is positive or negative, you need to know.
- **Set up a regular meeting with your manager:** Why not put the final element of your performance plan in place by establishing a monthly meeting with your manager? Not only would such a meeting help your visibility, it would be the perfect opportunity to review work expectations, to present the details of your telecommuting activities, and to receive feedback on the results.

At first glance, this may seem like a lot of extra work. In reality, adopting these habits and tips can help you maintain the highest performance rating you can, no matter what kind of work you do or where you do it. And, being skilled at building an excellent working relationship with your manager can assure an excellent performance history and perhaps a solid letter of recommendation, which are useful as you explore opportunities in the future.

Preparing Yourself for Opportunities in the Future

Success used to be measured in years with the company. My dad retired from Illinois Bell after working with the company for 38 years, a common occurrence for those who started their careers in the late forties and fifties. Even in the sixties and seventies, to have three employers in 10 years was considered job-hopping. In the late seventies, when I was promoted to product manager after 7 years with the company, I was near the bottom with seniority. But as you know, times have dramatically changed.

If in 5 years you are in the same job, you may be viewed by some as becoming position-stagnant. It is common for people to not only change jobs in 2 to 5 years, but also to change employers. During the dot-com frenzy, there was even a category of worker called the "heat seeking workforce" composed of employees who tended to change companies when their current employer's stock went down.

What kind of job will you have next? Will it be in a different department with your current employer? Will it be with a different employer? Will you go out on your own? How are you positioning yourself for your next career move? What are hiring managers looking for in the ideal employee these days?

No matter where your career takes you, remember that telecommuting prepares you well for your next job, and it should be a prominent line item under experiences in your resume. What kinds of opportunities are out there for you? Let's take a look.

Until the economy takes a serious downward turn, there will have never been a better time to seek employment than now, especially as an experienced telecommuter. In this era of technology-driven shift and radical workplace transformation, the power telecommuter must remain prepared to make chameleon changes to take advantage of opportunities. Opportunities abound for the individual who remains aware of changes, who becomes a student of his or her repercussions in the workplace, and who acquires the ability to predict these changes. Following are some signs of the times that are determining the types of workers in demand and how hiring decisions are being made.

- **Assemble a team of really good people and then make a plan:** There are so many opportunities in the communication age that the latest trend is to assemble a first-rate team and then put together a plan. In November 1999, Keyur Patel, then an executive at KPMG Consulting, saw the potential for business in the wireless market. He formed a company named Brience with individuals who are now the CEO, the head of operations, and the head of technology; received $200 million in venture capital; and apparently only *then* did they develop the details of their business plan.

- **"The fear of failure is replaced by the panic of success":** That's how an Intel advertisement, which appeared in the August 2000 issue of *Fast Company* magazine, described today's "surge economy." This perspective assumes that success is inevitable for those who dare to step outside the norm, take some risk, and ride the surge of the new economy. As a power telecommuter, with the right idea and the right timing, you are uniquely positioned to think really big, assuming you want the burden of millions of dollars in your bank account!
- **Boat rockers may be best employees:** It used to be that employees who bucked the system were chastised because they didn't follow the organization's rules. Today, there is evidence that people who are known to rock the boat at the office may be the best employees. A study by Valerie Sessa, an associate at the Center for Creative Leadership in Greensboro, North Carolina, concluded that conflict can breed creativity, productivity, and motivation. The study results show that employees who had argued about job issues such as ethical dilemmas, scheduling problems, and administrative questions were more likely to be productive. "A little bit of conflict shakes a team up," said Sessa. "It gives them energy. It gets them to question their own assertion."
- **Employees are outliving their employer:** Keeping your skill set current is more important than ever. "For the first time in human history, people can expect to outlive the organizations that they work for," observed author Peter Drucker in an interview with *Fast Company*. "As we live longer and work for more years, we risk becoming 'too good' at what we do." Drucker explained. "Work that felt challenging when we were in our thirties may feel dull when we reach our fifties—at which point we have 20 years left in our careers."
- **Employers are listening to employees' needs:** In a tight labor market, competing employers are offering incentives like telecommuting to lure quality employees. "Job seekers have many choices in today's tight labor market and they are looking for employers that recognize they have lives outside the office," said

> Carol Sladek, a work/life consultant with Hewitt Associates, as reported in an interview with the *Seattle Post-Intelligencer*. "Employers know that in order to remain competitive, they need to offer benefits that help employees balance their work and personal lives."

Why are these trends important to you as a power telecommuter? Each of these trends adds to your information database, providing hints on what motivates hiring managers and perhaps where to set your expectations for your employer prospects. These are some of the market conditions that could shape your directions as you consider a variety of career paths in your future.

To position yourself on the leading edge of change, you must remain tuned-in to these and other workplace-transforming trends. If and when you do begin seeking employment outside your current employer, here is what hiring managers are looking for in candidates.

What Are Hiring Managers Looking For?

"Even in a tight labor market, hiring managers must be very particular about the type of person they hire for key positions," said Theresa Perry, president of Atlantek Network. "It takes more than just a resume listing the right buzzwords," said Perry, a recruiter who specializes in placing high-tech professionals. "This person must also fit well into the organization's culture." As you set your priorities for updating your personal skill sets, perhaps you should take a hint or two from the traits that hiring managers look for in the ideal candidate:

- Problem-solving skills
- Integrity and a strong work ethic
- Communication skills
- Team experience and leadership skills
- Self-confidence and enthusiasm
- Technology skills and willingness to learn

Notice I didn't mention experience. While it certainly goes without saying that an accountant must know accounting and a programmer must know programming, the trend is to look as carefully at the person as one does at the skill set. Employers are recognizing that if highly skilled employees don't support the corporate culture, they will likely contribute to a retention problem and enjoy much less success.

In Chapter 1, I present the traits you need as a new worker in the new economy. To survive, you need to broaden and update your knowledge base, develop a specialty skill having value to the organization, improve analytical and computing skills, and perhaps develop a new work ethic. As you consider your career directions and plans, you are faced with some very difficult questions. Let's take a look at some of these questions as you set priorities for updating your work skill sets.

Setting Priorities for Updating Your Work Skill Sets

You have more control over your destiny than you may believe. If you are already telecommuting, you are way ahead of the success curve. To advance at the rate you wish, you need to make sure that your work skill sets match those in demand in your field. As you make job and career plans, you must make an honest assessment of where you rate today, identify traits and skills that need improving, and make a plan to improve them. The following are the three skill set areas.

- **How well does your current position fit into the future?** Your job, your industry, and your career path will likely be affected by trends over which you have no control. How will workplace trends affect your work, salary, and survivability? Are you tracking the trends that are affecting your job, career, and livelihood? Is your position on the decline or will it be in greater demand? Will your life stage have a significant effect of your career path? The answers to these questions may cause you to look outside your current industry and result in major career path changes. If it does, perhaps you should solicit the guidance of a qualified career counselor so that you can make these decisions as objectively as possible.
- **Do you have the skills to thrive in the new workplace?** In Chapter 2, I describe the traits it takes to thrive in the new workplace. They are identical to the skills needed for successful telecommuting.

As you set your priorities for the future, you may wish to ask yourself the following questions: Are you adaptive and willing to change? Are you an excellent information manager? Do you have the drive and independence of the ultimate entrepreneur? Are you empowered as a team player? Are you positioned as a specialist critical to the organization? Are you an excellent communicator? These are skills and traits that can be acquired, learned, or at least dramatically improved through courses at your community college, in books from your local bookstore, or even on the Internet.

- **What are you doing to update your personal skill sets?** Students are graduating from college with a distinct advantage over seasoned workers. How will you bridge the gap between you and someone with great skills but no experience? How will you leverage telecommuting to enhance your resume, work accomplishments, and professional growth? How well have you defined and honed your skill sets? Are you keeping your technology skills current? Are your visionary skills regularly exercised? Have you established clear performance metrics for yourself? How are your organizational skills? What about your skill of persuasion? Are you becoming more self-reliant? Are your communication skills constantly being updated? Do you pride yourself on your ability to learn? Only you know the answer to these questions, and only you can make the changes in your life to improve or master the skills that you know are important for you to excel as a worker, as a professional, as a telecommuter.

As a power telecommuter, you should be asking these questions as you set priorities for updating your work skill sets. If you are interested in competing and advancing in today's changing, competitive work environment, you need to level the playing field by updating your skill sets. But what if your next job isn't a traditional job at all? Have you considered the option of "free agency" for your next position?

Your Current Job May Be Your Last

An increasingly popular alternative to traditional employment is being an independent contractor, dubbed the "free agent" by Daniel H. Pink in *Free*

Agent Nation: How America's New Independent Workers Are Transforming the Way We Live, published in 2001 by Warner Books. In December 1997, when Pink postulated his free-agent theory in *Fast Company* magazine, he estimated the existence of an entire workforce of people—perhaps 25 million of them—who "move from project to project and who work on their own, sometimes for months, sometimes for days." A majority of these free agents work from their homes. And a huge percentage of them probably used to work for somebody else before they ventured out on their own.

"Free agency provides what people want: freedom, authenticity, security, accountability, self-defined success," Pink said in his keynote address at the International Telework Association & Council annual conference in September 2000. "One of two people become a free agent when they receive a windfall," said Pink. "Boomers are about to inherit $10 billion. Imagine what that will do for free agency!" he exclaimed.

Does free agency sound right for you? You may want to look into it by reviewing the information and services provided by the many Web pages where free agents can seek work, including www.freelance.com, www.elance.com, and, of course, www.freeagent.com.

When you ask yourself what kind of work will you be doing in five years, free agency is an option worth considering. If you have the talent and skills that are in demand, and that's the path you wish to take, telecommuting will give you much of the training and experience you need to get there.

Telecommuter Career Path Strategies That Work

In a world where people change jobs as frequently as they change automobiles, the power telecommuter must keep career path options open to nontraditional directions. As the popularity of telecommuting grows, many new career opportunities and options will emerge. As more people are free to make home-location decisions that are no longer dependent on their work location, they will find themselves much more content with their lives. Let's take a look at various career path strategies, first based on your position goals and then strategies based on your location goals.

Career Path Choices Based on the Position

The primary drivers or limitations for engaging in telecommuting career path strategies are the type of job you have now or the skills you have (or will acquire) that are adaptable to a position outside your field. Here are some ways you could adjust your career path to include a telecommuting option.

- **Develop a specialty that is in high demand:** Many individuals are skilled and capable in a field that is in high demand by employers. An excellent example of this occurred near the end of the nineties when thousands of Y2K "experts" emerged into the marketplace and were hired by large employers. What specialties are in high demand? In a recent PBS series titled *Livelihood,* the fastest growing jobs in the United States from 1994–2005 include personal and home care aides, systems analysts, computer engineers, physical therapy aides, electronic pagination systems workers, physical therapists, residential counselors, human-services workers, occupational therapists, manicurists, medical assistants, paralegals, medical records technicians, special education teachers, amusement and recreation attendants, correction officers, and guards. Of course, you'll need to be sure to pick a position that can be mobile!
- **Choose a position that is traditionally mobile:** If you want an opportunity to telecommute, you could target one of the many jobs that are traditionally mobile. These jobs typically involve travel, such as sales, field service, site inspector, collections agent, lobbyist, and insurance claims adjuster.

"What is needed is a new definition of 'career' that focuses less on a progression up the ladder in a profession or corporation and more on recognizing opportunities and adapting. Rather than focusing on a one-career preparation path, current and future workers need a higher quality of education that integrates general knowledge in both the arts and sciences with emerging technology."

Edward E. Gordon, "Help Wanted: Creating Tomorrow's Workforce," *The Futurist*, July–August 2000

- **Work for a virtual corporation:** If you have a small company of knowledge worker professionals, why do you really need the expense and overhead of an office? Many companies are being formed and operating successfully with that philosophy. The employees meet and communicate regularly, and, if there is a need to make a customer presentation that will leave a lasting impression, they rent some professional space that provides those services. One such company is ExecutiveWorks Worldwide, with employees who work from their home offices. "As a virtual company," explained the narrative on the company's home page, "we have been able to acquire and retain top talent all across North America and elsewhere."
- **Seek employment with a telecommuting employer:** This is not as easy as it sounds for a variety of reasons. See more detail later in this chapter under "Tips for Finding a Telecommuting Job."
- **Conduct your own online job search on the many free telecommuting job sites:** There are seemingly hundreds of Web sites that promise a listing of telecommuting jobs. Before you start searching, however, read "What the 'Home-Based Jobs' Web sites Won't Tell You," later in this chapter.

Career Path Choices Based on the Location

Your home location can become primary driver behind a career path strategy. Here are a variety of career path strategies for the telecommuter that revolve around where you wish (or need) to live.

- **Live near where you work:** This option gives telecommuters the most flexibility. The term "near" is relative, though, and in this case simply means that the main office is close enough for a reasonable commute when you must be there.
- **Live where you want or need to live, and work for a distant employer:** More and more people are living outside the normal commute distance, requiring them to be considered full-time telecommuters. I've seen many cases where a spouse is transferred to a different city, and the other spouse is offered the opportunity to work for his or her current employer from home in the new city.

Although these "forced" telecommuting situations are not unusual today, the frequency of well-positioned, valued employees requesting such an arrangement will become more commonplace. Other reasons for this arrangement include needing to live near a parent requiring care, near a university to earn a degree, in a healthier climate to reduce the symptoms of an illness, and wanting to keep your home where it is even though your employer has moved.

- **Live where you want and become a free agent:** If you have the skills to provide a service that's in demand, and you have the entrepreneurial drive, talent, and guts, you are in the driver's seat. As discussed earlier, the home-based free agent is becoming more common. Many people have transitioned from employee to free agent by taking early retirement from their employer and being rehired, by becoming recognized in a particular field of expertise, by coming up with a brilliant, unique application or service that people need, or simply by being in the right place at the right time. Irrespective of how you get there, free agency can be a risky yet highly rewarding career choice.

"Now people work at night because someone else is working where it's not night."
James Burke, *The Day The Universe Changed,* The Discovery Channel

- **Work in a foreign country for firm based somewhere else:** Technology has advanced to the point that your work headquarters and home can be continents apart. If living in Europe, the Middle East, or Australia is a high priority for you, and you have the right job skills and a willing employer, what difference does it make where your employer is located? A variety of factors favor this arrangement, including very low overseas long-distance rates, the increase of 24/7 customer support (you could work as a customer service or technical support agent during the day there when it is night here), demand for skilled workers in foreign countries, and United States employers willing to do just about anything to hire highly skilled employees. For an excellent resource on the logistics in "expatriate and offshore

Internet telecommuting," take a look at www.escapeartist.com/tele/commute.htm.

As you can see, the opportunities for the ambitious, talented power telecommuter seem endless. But how do find these great jobs? The next section will help you with the opportunities and realities of landing a telecommuting job.

Tips for Finding a Telecommuting Job

With all the talk and growth statistics about telecommuting, you might think that it is fairly common among employers. However, formal telecommuting is relatively uncommon among mainstream employers. Many employers who say they allow telecommuting offer it under limited circumstances. Other employers believe telecommuting provides such a competitive advantage that they keep their program low profile. So, if you're not already telecommuting and you want to find a job with the option, how do you do it? Here are some tips for finding and landing that telecommuting job.

- **Base your expectations on reality:** If you're thinking someone's out there waiting to give you a legitimate, high-paying, home-based job, you may be kidding yourself. If you expect to begin telecommuting immediately after you are hired in a new position, you may be sadly mistaken. You can expect a waiting period before you can begin telecommuting in a new job, depending on the type of work and the employer's attitude toward remote work.
- **Apply for a position that is traditionally mobile:** Certain jobs are naturally more mobile, and if telecommuting is your top priority, you'll need to focus on one of those jobs. As mentioned earlier, these jobs normally involve travel, such as sales, field service, site inspector, collections agent, lobbyist, and insurance claims adjuster.
- **Find the job that matches your skills, and then see if telecommuting is an option:** Taking any job just because you can do it from home will end up making both you and your employer miserable. When looking for suitable employment, especially in a strong economy, first look for work that is in your field and at your skill

level. Then, if you find work that you really want to do, explore telecommuting options before you hire on.

- **Be sure telecommuting is listed as one of your requirements:** Don't spring your telecommuting request on your new boss after you've been hired. Be sure to make it very clear on your resume and in your interview that you intend to be a telecommuting employee.
- **Don't expect to telecommute right away:** Most telecommuting employers have a policy that requires an employee to be with the organization for a specific amount time (say six months to two years) before qualifying for telecommuting. The bottom line is, you should land the ideal job first and work out the telecommuting privilege later.
- **You may not telecommute at all:** Confirm that your prospective employer has a formal telecommuting policy and active program in place. Some employers have been known to advertise a telecommuting option but allow it only in rare situations. Make contact with someone in the company who is willing to describe the details about the telecommuting environment before you hire on.

Until telecommuting becomes a mainstream workplace alternative, finding a great job in your field with excellent pay and a telecommuting option may be difficult for a few more years. But don't give up. More and more employers are offering a telecommuting option and more and more legitimate resources are becoming available to match the demand for good workers with the supply. The next section reviews some of the truth and pitfalls of home-based jobs advertised on the Internet.

What the "Home-Based Jobs" Web Sites Won't Tell You

You've seen the roadside signs and the junk e-mail messages:

"Work part-time and earn up to $50,000"

"Put your computer to work and earn thousands"

"Earn $1,500 a month from home!"

The Internet has brought the saying "There's a sucker born every minute" to a new level. I receive unbelievable offers regularly, as I'm sure you do. The unbelievable offers for easy money from home-based work should be considered just that: unbelievable. The same pitches now appear on Web sites.

Clark Howard, a nationally syndicated consumer talk show host based at News Talk 750WSB in Atlanta, told his audience that he has yet to find a legitimate source for telecommuting jobs on the Internet. There are others that believe that some sites can be reliable resources. How do you decide which sites are legitimate? Many of the home-based-jobs Web pages don't tell you a variety of things. If you decide to try their services give these thoughts some consideration.

- **You don't have to pay for the information they're selling:** If the site's main product seems to be a list of anxious employers or some kind of "telecommuting job search kit" for a price, shy away from it. Usually, this information can be readily found on Web for free.
- **"Working at home" is the best part of the job:** Unless you are content with assembling jewelry or making cold calls to unwilling prospects, a pitch that focuses on working from home first and the type of work second is not designed for the power telecommuter and should be avoided.
- **The jobs in their database may not exist:** I've seen situations where the operators of these services copy ads at random from the newspapers and other sources to fill up their job listings. The opportunities are in many cases old, contrived, or filled by the time you get to them.
- **Any salary listed is often impossible to achieve:** It's easy to show testimonials where other "members" have made huge amounts of money, but the potential for this kind of success is often limited. Once again, if the salary seems unbelievable, it usually is.
- **Much of their advertising techniques are annoying or against the law:** A red flag should go up when the organization advertises with bulk e-mail or illegally placed signs on telephone poles and parkways. Bending the rules by using these methods to get their message out could be a sign of the moral foundation of all their business practices.

- **If "no experience is necessary" it's likely illegitimate:** What kind of legitimate work would require no resume, no work history, or no experience? Unless you are desperate for cash, the power telecommuter would never consider such a position.

You get the idea. If you watch for these and other signs that the situation doesn't add up, it probably doesn't. Keep in mind, too, that some of these Web pages are legitimately designed to meet a market demand and, as time goes on, more and more pages will genuinely serve a need.

Developing a Retirement Strategy As a Telecommuter

When you think about retirement, what kind of daily life do you envision? Do you see yourself relaxing on the golf course, piddling in the garden, watching television, reorganizing the attic, or repainting the living room? Or do you see yourself volunteering as a small business counselor, taking on a part-time job in a plant nursery, going back to school for another degree, or editing the newsletter for your favorite club?

Retirement means something different to different people. As a power telecommuter, your vision of retirement is probably about putting your energies into something important to you and something you have wanted to accomplish, create, or benefit from for a long time. How often have you heard retired persons tell you they are busier than ever? That's the kind of retirement that a true power telecommuter will have.

I like to look at telecommuting as training for retirement. If you analyze telecommuting and retirement, they share many traits. The main ones are control and flexibility. In telecommuting and retirement you have control over your schedule, your time, your day, and how you balance your priorities. In telecommuting and retirement you have the flexibility to rearrange your schedule and priorities to meet the needs of the moment. And for the most part, in telecommuting and retirement, you are independent of others' influence over these things, allowing you to the freedom to stay in control.

The driven and ambitious power telecommuter will tend to lead a more active retirement. So, my advice is to begin your own early retirement program. As you telecommute more, begin imagining yourself as retired, comfortable with your financial situation, and willing and able to accomplish anything you want on your own terms. Before you go too far into the future, though, you need to make sure you are well grounded in the telecommuting present. Since your success in retirement is so closely tied with the way you prepare, you need to make the most of your current telecommuting privilege.

Making the Most of Your Telecommuting Privilege

You must admit that being a power telecommuter is indeed a privilege. Within certain limitations, you have the freedom to work whenever and wherever it makes sense to get the job done. You've also seen that it comes with some cost. It requires discipline, organization, new habits, and cooperation from others. It requires a delicate balance and the ability to prevent excessive overlap of work, family, and personal time. Let's review some ways that the power telecommuter should make the most of today's telecommuting privilege.

- **Become a model of the new workplace:** It's one thing to follow trends and yet another to be a trendsetter. That's what the power telecommuter does. Stay aware of the changes in your workplace, in the workplace of your competitors and peers, and in the workplace of the leading organizations in the world. Be the first to begin applying these changes in your work and in your life, and you will remain successful in whatever you do.
- **Keep the telecommuting business case fresh:** No matter where you go and what you do, someone will question your telecommuting integrity. Track the benefits to yourself, quantify the telecommuting benefit to the organization, and regularly update your personal telecommuting business case so that you not only defend your telecommuting position but are admired for it.

- **Use your technology wisely:** Technology enables telecommuting, allowing knowledge workers to perform portable tasks whenever and wherever it is most conducive to higher productivity. Take advantage of the technology to become a successful employee.
- **Constantly fine-tune the balancing act:** There is no bigger challenge to the power telecommuter than to balance work and personal time. Keep all your senses open to symptoms of extreme swings either way. Listen to your spouse, your closest friends, and your manager. They will be the first to recognize an imbalance. When imbalance begins to occur, make an immediate effort to bring the situation back to center.
- **Make your home office your castle:** Your home office should be a place that you look forward to going to, are proud to show off, and yet are able to leave after a full day's work. It should be safe, secure, and adequately separate from family activities. Equip it with the things that will make you more efficient and keep it organized and neat. Find creative ways to reduce stress, overwork, and distractions.
- **Communicate better than you ever have before:** There's a reason I dedicated an entire chapter to effective communication. When you boil it down, all we have is communication. Focus on your fundamentals, practice good communication etiquette, use the appropriate communication media for the purpose, and find clever ways of being virtually visible.
- **Be sure you're fitting in while working away:** Solidify your telecommuting credibility by becoming a power telecommuter. Be sure to remain reachable and stay on the radar screen of those who matter. When working away, stay as visible as needed to keep the boss informed of your activities and to remain reachable without giving up quiet time. When there are signs it's time to visit the office, don't hesitate.
- **Remain vigilant in positioning yourself for the future:** The future of a power telecommuter holds so much potential that the biggest challenge you may have is deciding which opportunities to chase. Take the time to update your work skill sets so that whatever the future holds, you are prepared. You will have traditional and radical

career path strategies from which to choose, so r
your telecommuting privilege today to be even
the future.

Your success as a power telecommuter starts today, in the everyday experiences of remote work. Your future and success as a telecommuter depend on the effectiveness of the basic habits you develop, the daily decisions you make, and commitments you keep.

Clearing a Path for Telecommuting Success

As you read in Chapter 5, achieving success as a power telecommuter requires that you establish your own standards, set rules for others who have access to you, and refresh your plans regularly. You need clear daily goals, self-motivation, strong discipline, internal conviction, and dedication to success. As a worker, especially as a telecommuting worker, doing a good job everyday is the best way to prepare for the future.

One of the most important elements of success for telecommuting is deciding what work you intend to do in the remote location, and being fully prepared to carry out that work. Because of this, your telecommuting day will always begin the day before you work from home. You must determine what work items you will need and how you will make sure you have them. Here are some reminders for preparing well for your telecommuting day:

- **Make a to-do list with priorities:** The day before you telecommute, make a to-do list, set priorities for your workday, and review your plans with your manager. Use the forms in Chapter 2 to identify and track your telecommuting work activity.
- **Make a to-take list:** Make a list of the items you must bring with you with to perform the work. This list may include work files, office supplies, reference materials, contact numbers for key individuals, and so on. Refer to the checklist at the end of Chapter 4 for additional guidance.

- **Announce your intentions to telecommute to those who need to know:** Make sure your office buddy, key coworkers, and contacts know that you are telecommuting. Leave a "Gone Telecommuting" sign on your desk and leave a "working away from the office" message on your voice mail.
- **Stay in the loop and on the radar screen:** You learned in earlier chapters the dangers of disappearing as a telecommuter. Be sure to practice appropriate communication etiquette, stay in the loop while you are working away, stay on the radar screens of key people, and maintain virtual relationships, as described in Chapter 6.
- **Be technology prepared and communication connected:** Make a mental note of the technology tools and connectivity you will need to perform your intended tasks. Do you have the appropriate software? Is your hardware and office environment ready? Do you have a plan B in place in case of equipment failure? Are your battery operated devices fully charged? Do you have contact information for technical support? A quick review of Chapter 3 might be useful.
- **Effectively manage your workload:** To maximize the telecommuting day, have you set work priorities? Have you made arrangements not to be disturbed during certain times of the day? Have you accumulated extra tasks and assignments that are suitable for telecommuting in case you must spend an extra day or two at home? Perhaps this is a good time to review Chapter 5.
- **Plan your telecommuting day:** A benefit of telecommuting is flexibility. Your day plan can be as loose as you need, assuming you can accomplish your goals. If you need more structure to your day, outline a work schedule for the day including when you will retrieve messages, make return calls, check e-mail, take breaks, perform specific tasks, and so on. At the very least, you should block out periods of time for specific tasks and discipline yourself to accomplish them.
- **Record your accomplishments and share them with your manager on your return:** A key to maintaining your credibility is knowing and reporting what you accomplished during your telecommuting day. Take a moment to review "Making Sure the Boss Knows What You're Doing at Home" in Chapter 7.

- **Keep monthly records of your telecommuting activity:** Over time, your employer will want to know your telecommuting frequency, the purpose for your remote work and what was accomplished, changes in your performance, absenteeism, and other details. These records can be easily kept on the forms in Chapter 2.

Being consistently proficient at remote work is what becoming a power telecommuter is all about. It can help you flourish in your present position and prepare you well for other employment opportunities that may come your way.

Because you have come this far, there is little doubt that you are willing to make certain investments to become a successful telecommuter. Telecommuting is not easy, but like many other things worth working for, the benefits are highly rewarding. There is no doubt in my mind that your investment in telecommuting will pay off handsomely.

There is one thing you should always remember: If you were telecommuting, you'd be home now!

Telecommuter Resources on the Web

Magazines

Many quality magazines and periodicals are highly beneficial to the power telecommuter. Please see www.gilgordon.com/resources/magazines.htm for a comprehensive list and brief descriptions.

Books

The Canadian Telework Association site at www.ivc.ca/bookstore.html offers a comprehensive list of telecommuting books.

A detailed list of telecommuting books may be found at the home page of Fleming LTD telework consultants at www.mother.com/dfleming/dmflinks.htm.

Excellent telecommuting book resources are available from www.amazon.com. Search for "telecommuting" or "telework."

...uting Experts' Web Pages

...nsultant, trainer, and author and assist organizations in the ...pment and implementation of successful telecommuting programs. See my Web site at www.inteleworks.com.

Authors Paul and Sarah Edwards, long known for their many books and practical tips on working from home, can be found at www.paulandsarah.com.

Consultant John Edwards of Telework Analytics International implements distributed workforce programs and has developed highly effective telework software. See www.teleworker.com.

Consultant David Fleming provides links to "the best telework resources in the world" and a diverse collection of telecommuting writings at the commentary archives at www.mother.com/dfleming.

Author, consultant, and telecommuting guru Gil Gordon is known around the world as one of the foremost telecommuting experts. Gil offers priceless resources for telecommuters at www.gilgordon.com.

With four books on telecommuting, self-proclaimed "televangelist" June Langhoff offers excellent tips, news, and resources for telecommuters at www.langhoff.com.

As the father of telecommuting, Jack Nilles is a consultant, researcher, and author who provides a telework fundamentals overview and a telecommuting forecast at www.jala.com.

Journalist, speaker, consultant, and self-proclaimed "chief home officer" Jeff Zbar presents home office success stories, small office–home office (SOHO) resources, and plenty of useful tips at www.goinsoho.com.

Finding Work As a Telecommuter

The telecommuting guide at About.com supplies career tips, telecommuting job links, a newsletter, and weekly live forums to discuss telecommuting issues. It is available at telecommuting.about.com.

The Metro Atlanta Telecommuting Advisory Council (MATAC) provides tips and links for finding telecommuting jobs. See www.matac.org/Jobs/jobs.html.

General Telecommuting Resources

The NetworkWorld Net.Worker Web site and newsletter offer an excellent technical resource, an annual guide to "total networking power," and an Experts Exchange. Go to www.nwfusion.com/net.worker.

The YouCanWorkFromAnywhere.com newsletter and Web page offer links and articles to help you learn more about telecommuting and help you master your technology to be a better mobile worker. See www.ycwfa.com.

The Center for Urban Transportation Research specializes in research, technical assistance, education, and training on the community impact of telework and alternatives to driving alone to work. Find it at www.cutr.eng.usf.edu.

The Center for Office Technology (COT) offers a booklet titled "Setting Up a Successful Home Office" available at www.cot.org/hoffice.html. It provides tips and recommendations for setting up a safe, comfortable, and productive workspace at home.

The Ergonomics for Work Web page gives tips on ergonomics, health, and productivity at work and may be found at www.combo.com/ergo/index.html.

Associations

Home Office Association of America (HOAA) offers services to home-based and small business professionals and is found at www.hoaa.com.

The International Telework Association & Council (ITAC) provides its members with opportunities to network with other telecommuters and access to research and telecommuting educational activities. Find it at www.telecommute.org.

Mom's Home Work calls itself "The world's trusted link to careers at home." The organization's tips for working moms, links to related Web pages, and free online newsletter can be found at www.momshomework.com.

The Canadian Telework Association site at www.ivc.ca offers power telecommuters one of the most comprehensive telecommuting resources available, including relevant articles, case studies, and links.

Home Office Products and Services

There is no better resource for a comprehensive list of telecommuting services and products than Gil Gordon's Web page, www.gilgordon.com/resources/products.htm.

Consumer Protection and Education

For consumer protection and advice on buying just about any product or service for your home office, see www.clarkhoward.com.

Consumer Reports Online provides "unbiased ratings and recommendations" of nearly any home office product and is available at www.consumerreports.org.

Shareware, Freeware, and Software Evaluation Sites

An extraordinary amount of free or inexpensive software is provided online. Often called shareware, this software is available from www.shareware.com, www.filemine.com, www.softseek.com, www.topfile.com, and others.

Free Internet and E-Mail Services

Several organizations offer free or very low cost Internet or e-mail services, including www.bluelight.com, www.juno.com, www.altavista.com, www.netzero.com, and www.yahoo.com. For a listing of free Internet providers, see www.freeispsearch.com.

Cellular and Long-Distance Purchase Decisions

For help in making a decision on telephone service, see www.point.com.

For guidance on personal and business-to-business cellular services, see www.decide.com.

Security

The Computer Emergency Response Team (CERT) Coordination Center publishes a variety of security alerts at no charge and may be found at www.cert.org.

For an excellent resource for security solutions, definitions, and resources, click on "Links" at the Information Systems Security Association (ISSA) Web page at www.issa.org.

Key Terms Used in This Book and by Telecommuters

Buddy, main office. A trusted, dependable individual who keeps a power telecommuter informed of main office changes, announcements, rumors, and activities.

Closet telecommuter. A telecommuter with immediate management approval but whose organization has no telecommuting policy in place.

Commuter choice options. The term used by the Environmental Protection Agency to describe commuter alternatives to travel in a single-occupant vehicle. These alternatives include mass transit, carpooling, and telecommuting.

Creative work avoidance. Inventing excuses to engage in activities other than work.

Cross-functional relationships. Deliberate professional affiliations with individuals for the purpose of networking outside a worker's regular circle of contacts. The worker would not regularly interact with these individuals otherwise.

Day extender. An individual who extends the workday by working beyond normal hours away from the main office.

Desk sharing. More than one employee using the same desk, office, or workstation at different times during a day or week.

Digital blacksmith. A telecomputing expert who provides personal advice on technology decisions and the best tools for remote applications, and who remains on-call to troubleshoot technology problems. *See* **telecomputing.**

Driven knowledge worker. An independent, intelligent individual with an information-based position who tends to work at full capacity, sees obstacles as challenges, remains focused on success, and is good at balancing ambitious professional goals with personal and family goals.

Free agent. In the context of the new economy, an independent worker with specialized skills who moves from project to project on a demand basis.

Home agent. A corporate employee working as a reservations, telemarketing, customer service, or other such agent, typically full-time from home.

Hoteling. A program using a hotel-like reservation system that allows telecommuters to reserve and use shared office space on a temporary basis. Also known as **free address** and **territory-free office space**.

Infomediary. An individual or service that offers aggregated specialty services, intelligent purchase assistance, technology-based buying aids, or a community-based buying environment to assist consumers in making purchase decisions.

Just-in-time (JIT) workspace. Hoteling workspace. *See* **hoteling.**

Knowledge worker. An individual who works in an information-based position.

Mail screener. An individual who monitors a telecommuter's in-box at the main office for important deliveries such as announcements, airline tickets, software upgrades, security codes, and so on; notifies the telecommuter of such deliveries; and makes arrangements for the telecommuter to receive them.

Mentor. A well-placed individual in an organization or industry who provides professional counsel and guidance to help the telecommuter realize personal growth and development, make informed career decisions, and broaden professional networking opportunities.

Mobile worker. A telecommuter or teleworker.

New economy. The modern economic engine driven by electronically linked individuals and companies operating under new rules of time, space, efficiency, relationships, and economics.

New workplace. The work environment resulting from the new economy and characterized by any or all of the following: employee value is determined by contribution, talent, and fitting in; employees may also be owners and shareholders; work is accomplished in shared workspaces; work information is highly accessible electronically; employees are specialists in their field and involved in the entire process; attractive recruiting incentives are offered; and a casual, relaxed workplace is combined with play.

Nomadic employee. A road warrior. *See* **road warrior.**

Nonterritorial office. An office that utilizes some sort of workspace allocation program, which does not assign desks or workstations to specific individuals for any length of time.

Power telecommuter. A self-disciplined mobile worker who requires minimal supervision, is a skilled communicator, balances work and personal life, is an independent team player, manages time well, and stays in the loop while working away from the office.

Remote work center. Remote workspace usually used part-time by hoteling telecommuters. *See* **hoteling** *and* **telework center.**

Remote worker. A telecommuter.

Remote work satchel. A carrying case that contains the telecommuter's files, data, reference materials, contact information, and other critical items needed to work remotely.

Road warrior. An employee who operates from a virtual office. *See* **virtual office.**

Satellite offices. Office centers, such as regional sales offices or district service centers, typically used full-time by employees who live near them.

Telecommuter pledge. A personal commitment by the power telecommuter to take telecommuting to a professional level.

Telecommute/Telecommuting. A combination of remote and office-based work by an employee, facilitated by communication technology. *See* **telework.**

Telecommuting agreement. The basic "contract" that establishes telecommuting terms and conditions for telecommuters.

Telecomputing. The process of combining computers, software, and communication networks to allow flexible alternatives to the traditional office.

Telefficiency. Improving organizational efficiency through the use of telecomputing technology. *See* **telecomputing.**

Telehermit. A telecommuter who becomes disconnected from important workplace activities and events.

Telemanager. An individual who is trained and responsible for managing remote workers. *See* **remote worker.**

Televillage. A community that combines education, health care, business development, and governmental services, some of which are connected electronically through videoconferencing. This allows high-speed transmission of pictures and words between residents and businesses.

Telework center. A remote workspace usually used part-time by hoteling telecommuters. Same as **remote work center.**

Telework/Teleworking. The act of working in a location away from a main office. Included are telecommuting, hoteling, working in a satellite office or remote work center, and working from a virtual office. Frequently synonymous with telecommute/telecommuting. *See* **telecommute.**

To-take list. A list prepared by a telecommuter the day before working remotely to assure that everything needed for telecommuting is gathered.

Touchdown area. Quiet areas in the main office designed for quick data downloads, telephone calls, and checking messages.

Transparent telecommuting. Working in a remote location that is irrelevant or unknown to those with whom the telecommuter interfaces.

Ultimate entrepreneur. A technology-enabled individual who exploits opportunities to deliver skilled services equivalent to larger providers but with much lower overhead.

Viral marketing. A method of online promotion in which a message is passed from one individual to another in much the same way that a computer virus replicates, sometimes multiplying itself at every receipt.

Virtual corporation. A business organization in which all or most employees work from their homes or in a remote location and where communication is predominantly or completely through electronics.

Virtual office. A work arrangement or situation that allows an individual the freedom and technology to work anyplace feasible for completing work.

Virtual relationship. A business relationship in which face-to-face interaction is minimal, if at all, and where communication is predominantly or completely through electronics.

Virtual team. A work team of individuals who are connected through a project or work responsibilities but who do not necessarily work in the same physical location.

Index

A

B

C

D

E

F

Q

R

S

U

V

W

Y

Z